Selling on the Extra Mile

by

Charles Householder

Householder Publishing Company
A Division of Householder Enterprises, Inc.

Householder Jr., Charles K. (Charles Keith), 1974—
Selling on the Extra Mile
1st edition

ISBN-13: 978-1481142908

ISBN-10: 1481142909

Acknowledgements

Writing this book is a project I have been intending to do for a long time, and I am grateful that it is finally complete. Thank you to my friend and colleague, Eric Meyer for the cover design, editorial advice, and for partnering with me on this and several other projects.

I am grateful to my father, Chuck Householder Sr., who invested his time in teaching me at an early age the skills of selling, and to my business mentor, Dick Minervino, who continues my sales training this very day.

Thank you to the many customers who serve as anecdotes in this book and to the profession of selling which has allowed me to enjoy many fun and unique adventures.

Thank you to my mom, Kathy, who didn't get a fair shake in my previous book, for all you do for me, and for continuing to support me in my various endeavors.

Of course, thank you to my wife, Sandra, who supports me daily, raises our daughter, and who willingly serves as a sounding board for all of the ideas and concepts, which have made their way into the following chapters.

Table of Contents

Introduction

Being able to sell, to really sell effectively, can dramatically improve many areas of your life both personally and of course professionally. Being able to sell others your ideas can rapidly propel your career forward. In fact, if you can sell yourself and your ideas, there is no limit to what doors can open for you. If you are reading this book and are a sales professional who gets paid in direct proportion to how well you can sell, then the more effective you are at selling, the more money you can earn, the more people you can help, and the greater success you can enjoy.

What's great about learning to sell effectively, and by effectively, I mean being able to maximize every single appointment and to close every possible sale, is that regardless of your education, your background, or even your previous work history, learning and applying the ideas contained in this program can immediately enhance the quality of your life. This is the beauty of the sales profession. Plus, if you are already experiencing success, being more effective in selling will increase your results and ultimately your rewards. Learning how to sell your products, services, ideas and yourself will put you on the fast track to success regardless of where you currently may be standing.

I want to commend and thank you for purchasing this book. In this highly competitive marketplace, the professional salesperson must keep enhancing their craft. Unfortunately, too few salespeople commit to ongoing training and development of their skills. As a result they find themselves dealing with regular slumps, erratic sales results, and frequent job frustration. However, by committing to a philosophy of continual growth and improvement, and then reinforcing that commitment by studying books such as this one, you can immediately separate yourself from your peers and rise above the competition.

This book is for anyone desiring to be wildly successful in sales. Whether you're selling cars, insurance, real estate, electronics, telephones, memberships, you name it; whether you are selling any product or service, to individual consumers or large and small businesses alike; this unique book and the philosophy it contains can help you to sell more and perform better than your competition.

By the way, if you are not directly employed in a sales specific role you are still going to want to read this book and practice the techniques found herein. Because the fact is everyone must sell. You have to sell yourself in a job interview, sell your ideas to your boss, sell yourself to the opposite sex, and sell your supervisor on why you deserve a raise. Even if you are an author, the action word in "best-selling book" is *selling*.

Growing up, I was raised in an environment in which I held the sales profession in very high esteem. For this reason, I was anxious to begin my professional career in selling as soon a possible. Immediately in my first selling role, I came to find out that there is a proven statistic in the sales industry which demonstrates that: 20% of salespeople in any organization produce 80% of the total sales for that organization. This statistic intrigued me, and it fueled my desire to discover what the 20% did to become successful that the remaining 80% did not. As a result, I spent the next twenty years on the front line gaining firsthand experience selling a variety of products and services, often in environments where my only source of income came from the products I sold. I am talking about 100% commission, limited support, "make or break" environments. Fortunately,

2

thanks to my foundational training and my commitment to constantly expanding my skills, in almost all cases I flourished!

The materials presented in the following pages are the best sales techniques, strategies, and concepts that I have discovered in those past twenty years of practical research.

In this book, you are in fact going to learn what the 20% of sales professionals do in order to guarantee their continued success. Intertwined throughout these teachings are the combination of psychology (because as you may already know and will definitely come to realize, selling is very much a mental game), and specific habitual actions. In each chapter you'll come to understand what the very best do to succeed daily, such as their mindset, how they spend their time, and how they structure their business.

Plus, all the teachings in this book are wrapped around a timeless philosophy that is practiced mainly by the elite sales professionals the world over. In the following pages you will discover that philosophy and how you can immediately apply it to your business as well. I can confidently say, this book *Selling on the Extra Mile* can be your most valued guide to success in selling.

Selling on the Extra Mile

Why the title Selling on the Extra Mile? For two reasons: first, this is the philosophy my first mentor (who happens to be my father) instilled in me when I was just beginning my selling career, and it helped me to rise to the top of my company very rapidly. The second reason is that this wisdom contains a timeless truth that was imparted over 2,000 years ago. The phrase *"to go the extra mile"* is Biblical. Although, I don't claim to be an expert on the Bible by any means, I do know that during one of the greatest presentations in history, one that built an entire church, the wise presenter said, "and, whosoever shall compel thee to go a mile, go with twain."

So what does this actually mean and how does it apply to selling? You are going to learn specifically that in this book beginning with the first chapter.

You will come to understand why I chose to build my entire career on this philosophy of going the extra mile, and how I have shared this wisdom with many others in my current role as a sales trainer and coach, and as a result those people have also skyrocketed their careers with this training, while others have been able to turn around and improve entire companies.

As the name might suggest, this program is not just about doing more, but is also about setting larger goals, gaining more skills, becoming more as a person, and playing a bigger game at work as well as in life.

I believe that Selling on the Extra Mile is the only way to succeed in the 21st century. In this economy where companies rise and fall over night, and new products become obsolete shortly after they hit the market, this is the only certain method to guarantee your staying power, your growth, and your company's success.

My First Selling Mentor

Before we get into the heart of this program, let me share with you how I first came to learn and develop the Selling on the Extra Mile philosophy. Believe it or not, as a child I grew up in an environment where selling was prized. In the same way that children are encouraged from a young age to perhaps one day become a doctor, lawyer, or even President, in my house selling was held in the same high esteem. The reason for this was because my father, who grew up very poor, so poor that his family would goes days without regular meals, was able to rise out of the bonds of poverty by building a successful career in selling.

At the age of eighteen, after graduating from high school, my father was expected by his family to take a job working in the coal mines in Southeastern Ohio, where he grew up. However, he definitely did not want to do that and made it abundantly clear. So his parents kicked him out of the house and told him to go make a living on his own. Harsh!

Desperate for work, the best job he could get at the time was selling cameras in a local department store. Fortunately, he was a quick learner and had a

4

knack for selling, combined with a strong desire to succeed. In no time, he was successful in camera sales, and was promoted to department manager and then eventually store manager.

As a store manager, my father found success in turning around failing stores located in Ohio. As a result, he was promoted to take on and turnaround other stores across the Northeast that also hadn't been doing so well. After traveling to different stores to turn them around, he was eventually transferred to a retail store in Bridgeport, Connecticut, where he met the woman who would go on to be his wife and my mom. Shortly thereafter they got married, and I was born. Around that same time he was promoted to the role of district manager for a handful of retail stores and was then transferred from Connecticut to the state of Delaware.

This was a very difficult time for our family, especially my mom who had to move away from her family and everyone she knew with her first newborn and adjust to a new living environment.

Professionally however, my father continued to excel and was soon promoted to a Regional Manager role and transferred yet again to Cleveland, Ohio. There he was responsible for leading a chain of department stores. This promotion had him on the road much of the time while my mom was at home. To compound the distance, my mom didn't know anyone in Cleveland and was very lonely. Eventually she expressed to my father how she longed to return home to Connecticut. However, if my father decided to move back, this would mean that he would have to leave retail or take a major demotion to go to work with a competing store.

My father did a very honorable thing and resigned from his position, and they relocated us back home. For the next two months, we lived with my grandparents while he looked for a new job, which included considering work in a different industry.

One day, he saw a chance advertisement in the local newspaper looking for automobile salespeople for a growing family dealership. He interviewed and got the job and began his new career selling cars. Over the next twenty years he rose to the top of that same dealership making his mark in the automotive industry. The rapid trajectory of his climb in which he grew from the role of Salesperson to Used Car manager, New Car manager, and eventually General Sales manager for the entire store encompassing three major brands, can be traced directly to the *Selling on the Extra Mile* philosophy.

Note: I want to mention that it isn't all that common for a person in the automotive industry to stay with the same dealership for that length of time. Often salespeople will hop from dealership to dealership throughout their career. I think the fact that my father became a fixture at that family dealership demonstrates the proof of how he built his career based on integrity and giving fair deals; and how people continued to come back and buy from him again and again.

Everyone is in Sales

Like most kids, growing up I wanted to be like my dad. I can vividly remember being around five or six years old and tying a neck tie around my neck while standing next to my dad looking at our reflection in the mirror, and then going off to sell my grandparents the little motorized toy car I had. At that time, I dreamed of one day following in my dad's footsteps working in car sales. However, as I grew older, it appeared that my life was going into an entirely different direction. At age thirteen, I embarked on training in the martial arts and this helped me to completely transform my life. I recount this experience in my book *Warrior of Life: A Guide to Self-Transformation* which is currently available on AMAZON and at http://www.warrioroflife.com

Around my mid-teens, I decided that after graduating high school, I was going to own and operate my own martial arts school. Instead, my parents ultimately helped encourage me to go on to college to pursue a degree in interpersonal communication. While attending college, I did operate my own martial arts school within the local YMCA. It was during that time, while building my small business, that I made a discovery which would shape my future business perspective.

Essentially, I discovered that even though I thought my job was teaching martial arts, my real position was "sales and marketing" in the role of martial arts instructor. Because in order to succeed as an instructor, I had to sell parents on signing up their kids, and I had to sell adults on taking my classes. Plus, I had to continually market the various classes and programs I was offering to gain interest in the surrounding community to attract new students. From this experience, I was reminded just how important possessing selling skills was to determining a person's success in life. By the way, in this book, you will learn how you too, are a sales and marketing professional in the role of_____.

While teaching the martial arts for several years, I realized how I wanted to make a bigger contribution to how well a person's life turned out beyond their martial arts training. So I made the decision that I wasn't going to spend my career as a martial arts instructor, but rather would seek to become a professional speaker, teacher, and trainer. People have often asked me, "why didn't you start doing that right then?" The reason I believe is because in the martial arts you have to earn the right to become an instructor. I felt that I needed to be the equivalent of a *black belt* in personal development and sales training before I could think of offering this material to the public. This may be a manifestation of my own limited thinking at that time; however, this decision has served me well throughout my career. So immediately after graduating college, three days later to be exact, I took a job working for my dad at the local car dealership, with the intention of learning how to sell effectively so I could one day teach this material; along with the mental training I had learned through the martial arts.

My First Sales Job

Working for my dad had a major positive impact on me because he was equally as committed to my success as I was. Part of his commitment may have had a little to do with pride, being that he was not going to let his own son fail in this role. To help me succeed he continually shared with me all the knowledge in selling which he had accumulated during his lengthy career. In this book, you will learn the specific wisdom he shared as he imparted over thirty years of his selling success to me.

7

Because my early goal had been to share these success strategies, in those early years, I sought to gain as much varied experience as possible. After three years of success in auto sales, I took a position in Business to Business selling (B2B) working for a leading recruiting firm performing recruiting and staffing sales. At that particular staffing firm, the company had a rule that everyone had to recruit first and ideally *earn* a spot on the sales team. By applying the human relations techniques you will learn in this program, I was promoted to sales in six months (the average was two years). By applying the human relations training I had received while getting a degree in interpersonal communication and studying every book I could find on the subject, I was able to help people who were afraid to move from the position they had to the one they were offered and were thinking of backing out. I would help them to confront those fears and get them to make the decision to change. I am going to share some of those same influencing techniques in this book, such as how I got people to pull the trigger to move careers; and earlier when I was selling cars, to make a decision to buy autos.

After reading many books on selling and deciding to follow in the footsteps of those authors, I switched careers from recruiting and moved into financial planning and mortgage sales where I applied these same strategies with equally satisfying results.

To date, I have enjoyed success selling automotives, recruiting services, insurance and mortgages, as well as six figure marketing/PR programs to companies across the country. All the while studying everything I could get my hands on about personal development and selling, from books to audio programs and from attending seminars. Throughout my career I have studied and chronicled the best information and then tested it by applying it daily in my selling roles.

So I could make a positive difference, a few years ago I made the decision that I was ready to share these teachings with others professionally, so I began my speaking and coaching practice. Currently, I offer live sales training to companies and the public, and now I am excited to bring this information to you with this book.

As you will discover in these pages, I have plenty of anecdotal experiences having been there and done that. Along the way, for example, while getting my licenses in financial planning, I worked in a call center. I would spend my weeknights calling homeowners (often while they were having dinner) to sell them on life insurance. Just imagine how friendly those folks were to me. Yet, I was very successful, and was often called upon to share my skills with my peers at the agency.

I've also travelled the country, hopping planes, and living on the road selling products and services to various companies. So I know firsthand, what it takes to succeed in differing sales environments, and am grateful to be sharing those strategies with you.

One more thing, it is my belief that selling should change the salesperson. By adopting the teachings in this book, **you** should become better in all areas of life. How well you relate to people will get better. Your psychology and attitude will become more positive, your vocabulary will be more optimistic, and you will use words like "opportunity" instead of "problem." You will treat people better. You'll listen better. You will learn to ask for the order in sales, and likewise in your personal life you will ask for upgrades, promotions, and raises. Your negotiating skills, presenting and speaking skills will also improve as you immerse yourself and master the skills of selling. This book is your guide to cultivating all of these positive changes and results in your life.

My suggestion is to read this book again and again. Practice the strategies it contains. Selling is a skill and like any skill you must practice to get good. In business as in life, either you are growing and getting better, or you are stagnating and getting worse. There is no staying the same. My hope is that this book will be the vehicle to help you grow, become more, and achieve all of your goals through selling.

Section 1

Five Key Concepts

In the introduction, I mentioned how when I began working at the auto dealership, my father was committed to helping me succeed. After thirty years of success in sales, he had combined incredible insights into a practical philosophy on selling. The early things he taught me in my first professional selling role, automotive sales, continue to help me to succeed.

In this section you will discover the five key concepts he shared with me, which I expanded to suit my other selling careers. These five concepts lay the foundation for this book and for building a comprehensive understanding of what it takes to ultimately succeed in sales and business.

Chapter One

Key Concept #1

What you initially lack in skill you must make up for in activity.

Intrinsic in this first concept is the philosophy of expending more energy to create a positive difference in your results. This is expertly stated in the following passage taken directly from the New Testament in the Bible, "and, whosoever shall compel thee to go a mile, go with twain." For our purposes, the *whosoever* is the customer. Whatever they ask for, you want to deliver more than they could ever expect. This timeless truth in a nutshell is the mindset of the top salespeople; a mindset that you too are going to want to cultivate.

This concept of delivering more up front forms the basis of the Selling on the Extra Mile philosophy. It suggests doing more than is expected of you. Delivering more in value than the customer expects, and doing more than the competition is willing to do.

"For our purposes, the whosoever is the customer. Whatever they ask for, you want to deliver more than they could ever expect."

Too often in sales roles, even experienced salespeople will be engaged in many low value activities, or activities with no value at all. These individuals don't plan their days, instead choose to arrive at the office and let the day unfold on its own. As a result they achieve much less than they are capable of achieving. In addition, new salespeople are often relegated to shadow these individuals and soon they too develop the same bad practices, perpetuating a cycle of minimal effort and lackluster results. However, this need not be the case. With the philosophy of performing more activity in the forefront of the salesperson's mind, every customer interaction presents an opportunity to over deliver thereby providing high value. In addition, gaining new prospective clients becomes an ever increasing opportunity to ramp up performance and create and improve best practices.

In my first few days selling cars, my father said to me, "Chuck, a seasoned salesperson typically sells 3 out of every 10 customers they meet." "If with your limited experience, you can only sell 1 out of 10; and if you are going to be able to compete, you need to meet with 30 prospective customers for every 10 the other salespeople see. If you do this, then you'll win!" By win he meant to grow, succeed, and excel in selling.

The mandate was clear. If I was going to succeed, I had to see 3x the amount of people the other salespeople were meeting. I committed to this goal and sought out methods which allowed me to get in front of more customers on a regular basis. By doing this, my skills improved faster because I was presenting to more people and gaining more experience. Soon I was selling 2 out of 10, then 3 out of 10, and so on…

Too often, in sales organizations, new salespeople will join who possess much enthusiasm and they will initially see more customers than the other salespeople. However in the majority of cases they slow down their activities consistent to the average among the group.

The key to this philosophy is to see more prospective customers than your peers and the competition and then to keep up this level of activity. Never slow down! The universe rewards growth and expansion, and if you are going to enjoy the rewards of selling you must be constantly expanding your business, your influence and your reach. This is what going the extra mile is all about!

The following strategies are designed to assist you in seeing 3x more customers than you see now. Apply them immediately and watch your results grow:

Arrive Early

I once read the following quote by Michael Masterson the author of *Automatic Wealth* and *Ready, Fire, Aim* which said, "Getting to work early is such a common virtue of successful people, that I'm tempted to call it the single most important thing that you can do to change your life."

The hallmark of successful people is that they choose to arrive early. To separate yourself from the rest, you too need to get to the store or office earlier than everyone else does, or be out visiting prospects at their office early in the morning. Get a jumpstart to extra mile achievement by getting started early, staying late, and doing more than your peers.

In my experience when trying to reach C-level decision makers such as the CEO by telephone, they are most often accessible early in the morning before normal business hours. By calling at this time you are able to avoid the staff members often referred to as "gatekeepers" allowing you to contact the targeted individual easily and directly.

Food for thought, the fact that CEO's are often more reachable early in the morning begs the question, do they arrive early because they are CEO or are they CEO because they arrive early?

One additional reason to arrive early is that it orients your day in a positive direction. Planning to arrive early prevents you from being late even if you encounter a traffic jam on the way to your intended destination. When you arrive at the office early you will also notice that most of your colleagues haven't arrived yet, and the quietness provides a tranquil environment to prepare your mind for the day's activities; and it presents an environment free from distractions as you unleash your onslaught of phone calls on the potential marketplace.

Note: Don't just read this for entertainment. Successful salespeople **act when the idea is fresh and the inspiration is high**. When you read a strategy for your success in this book, take a moment and determine how you can implement it immediately. For example, make the decision now to arrive at your office tomorrow morning thirty minutes early; or, schedule a breakfast meeting with a prospect or networking partner. Whichever you choose, write it down in your calendar and commit to it now!

If you did this, **congratulations!** You are guaranteeing your future success.

Plan the Sales Day, the Night Before

The top selling professionals know that each sales day begins the night before. This means that before you leave the office at the end of the working day, take a moment and write out your plan for the very next day. Ideally, list the six most crucial activities you plan to perform the following day. In addition, plan your specific prospecting and follow-up calls. If necessary confirm the next day's appointments. Most importantly, do not rush out of the office at the end of the day, instead plan the next selling day in detail to ensure your continued success.

This idea of writing the top six crucial activities each night was introduced to Charles Schwab when he was running Bethlehem Steel in 1903 (and was recounted by Dale Carnegie). Essentially, Schwab's business consultant boasted that he could improve productivity at the company by 50%. The consultant then invited Schwab to test this claim by having his executive staff write each night before leaving work, the crucial six activities they each planned to accomplish the next day. If this worked to improve productivity by at least 50%, agree to pay him what Schwab thought the advice was worth. In just only two weeks, Schwab sent him a check for $25,000. Schwab later credited this very practice with helping him to transform Bethlehem Steel into a company worth over 100 million dollars.

16

Arriving early and *planning your day* the night before go hand in hand. In my own selling experience, I have noticed that in most cases, the unsuccessful people arrive at the office just on-time or late. Then, they spend the next forty-five minutes deciding what they are going to do that day. By the time they've started performing any selling related activities, countless precious hours have already been wasted.

The first thing you need to commit to in order to guarantee your success is that you must arrive early, and next be already prepared to work when you arrive because you planned your activities the previous night.

Be First in Everything

Be the first to arrive, the first to call customers, and the first to see customers. Make this your mantra "I will be first". First in activity usually equals most in results (provided it is continuous)!

One purpose of this strategy is to build momentum. When a rocket ship leaves Cape Canaveral en route to outer space, it expends most of its fuel at liftoff. However, once it has gained flight, momentum and the different environment (no gravity) help propel the ship to its destination. Just like a high powered rocket ship, your strategy is to invest your energy in being first. Once you get going, then you allow the momentum of activity and the opportunities it presents you to maximize your day.

One other thing, if your company or organization runs sales contests, decide immediately that you are going to do whatever it takes to win every contest. Settle for nothing less than first place!

There is No Second

A few years ago there was a movie starring Will Ferrell called *Talladega Nights*. In this movie, the main character grows up to be a race car driver in the hopes of being just like his dad (sounds familiar). What carries him

17

along in this pursuit is a maxim his dad spouted to him as a youngster, which is, "if you are not first, you're last." Later in the movie, when he meets up with his dad, his dad apologizes for misleading him, telling him that there is also a second, and third place, etc.

That might be true in racing, in golf, and other sports, whereas when you come in second you still go home with some of the rewards. However, this is not the case in selling. If you and several other competing salespeople are vying for a contract, and you find out that it has come down to you and just one other competing person, if the customer doesn't choose you to award the contract to, what are you left with? The answer is nothing.

In sales, second doesn't pay. The good news is this presents an opportunity. While most salespeople are satisfied giving it their perceived best shot, the Extra Mile Salesperson commits to doing whatever it takes to land the sale. So in addition to the maxim, "if you are not first, you are last," consider inculcating in your mind the affirmation, "I do more than they (the customers, competition, peers) could ever expect."

"If you are not first, you're last."

As you will see again and again throughout this book, going the extra mile means doing more than the prospect could ever expect and will likely not receive from your competition.

Be High Touch

One of the keys to gaining the initial sale, and then to attracting follow-up sales and renewals, is maintaining a position in the forefront of the prospective customer's mind. In this book, we will discuss many strategies for doing this including the following:

Send hand-written personal notes. In the digital age, sending personal notes is a great way to separate yourself from the competition, and to make the prospective customer feel important. You can send personal notes in the form of thank you cards, birthday, holiday, and anniversary cards. Simply, record the basic client information such as their birthday or anniversary into your calendar or calendar software, and then take the time to send them a hand written card to celebrate their particular milestone.

A similar strategy is to pay close attention and to take note of what your customers say during the actual sales call; what are their interests, what are they in to? Then send them books or magazine articles that are related to their interests.

Host events and invite your customers. Take your best customers to games and shows. Include them in holiday parties and other related functions. Build a relationship with your customers. Get to know them and you might find out as an added bonus who they know that might be a candidate for your products or services.

"Friend" them using social media such as Facebook and LinkedIn, and keep them up to date on various promotions and incentives your company offers by featuring those incentives through this medium. In fact, if you are not currently taking advantage of free platforms such as Facebook and LinkedIn to communicate with your prospects and customers, you are missing a huge opportunity.

Fortunately, many sales organizations are utilizing these tools and building a loyal following in the process. One car dealership here in Connecticut, is constantly posting pictures of the pre-owned cars they acquire in trade. More times than not I have found myself considering one of the high end vehicles they've showcased on their Facebook page.

Another dealership in Connecticut took a different more costly approach. They paid cable television to allow them to host a weekly show where they featured various pre-owned vehicles over the TV. Not only is this expensive, it can also be difficult to interact with the viewers. Alternatively, this could have been done for a fraction of the cost using YouTube and then marketed to individuals who were actually in the market for a new vehicle. The lesson is, be high touch and use these free tools!

Target Orphan Customers

When I went to work in the auto dealership, I put a system in place to send a letter to past customers who were referred to as "orphan owners." These were the customers whose previous salesperson had left the dealership in the time following the customer's last purchase. Each and every day, I would mail at least ten letters, one to each orphan owner, and then a few days later, in the evening, I would make a follow-up call to each person. This worked amazingly well for me and helped me to build my initial customer base. Once I connected with someone by phone, I would gather information about their buying habits and their interests, and then put them on a regular mailing of dealership promotions. Also, I'd send them a birthday and/or anniversary card at the appropriate time. The results from these combined activities were staggering. I cannot count how many times I would be summoned to the showroom to meet a customer who came to see me as a result of this approach. My suggestion is for you to apply this in your own business immediately. Identify the orphan customers of your company, and put a system in place for you to regularly reach out to them to encourage them to buy from you and your company again and again.

The reason this practice works so well is because in many cases, customers can be very *change averse* thus making them loyal to a particular brand or product by default. If you are not the only game in town, make sure they consider you by your building a system of frequent communications in the form of emails, letters, newsletters, postcards, phone calls, greeting and holiday cards, and other social media campaigns.

Note: I must stress that thanks to the increase in social media and the ease of use of various technologies, it is imperative you reach out to your customers in a variety of formats. For example, email them reminders, send them your quarterly e-newsletter (what? You don't have an e-newsletter? It only takes a few minutes to initially create and then can be used again and again), post relevant material online frequently that will be of interest to your customer base. The possibilities are limitless.

24/7 Professional

This mindset is perhaps the most critical, and is usually the number one determining factor between the most successful and the least successful people in sales.

Successful salespeople don't separate their business from the rest of their life. Successful people don't compartmentalize. Their business role is part of the fabric of who they are. Now, there is a time for conducting business and a time for other valuable activities. Don't be working on a business project every Saturday evening when you committed to spending time with your family. However, for a majority of the time, be thinking and talking about your business.

This was my father's approach, which worked exceedingly well, especially in his early years selling cars. When he began selling cars, he found himself building a career in a different state from the one he grew up in, in an unfamiliar community where he did not know many people. To succeed he had to be selling and marketing his business all of the time. As a result, he would tell anyone who would listen about the value his dealership could bring. As a result, he attracted customers at restaurants, on the golf course, and at his kid's sports games. He was always inviting people to the dealership to buy a car.

I too have kept this philosophy alive in my own career. Funnily, if you sit next to me on an airplane, I am going to try to sell you something. Seriously though, cultivating a passion for your product, service, and business is a key to manifesting success in your life. Being passionate is crucial, and if you are not passionate about what you are selling, find something else to sell which you can be passionate about. Because when you are passionate about what you are selling, then you will want to share it with everyone all the time! Make no mistake, I am not suggesting that you "puke" up all the features of your product or service to everyone you meet, what I am suggesting is that your antennae are always up, and you are always at the ready to give a welcoming description of what your company offers.

A big part of the magic of sales is a *transfer of enthusiasm*. Because you are knowledgeable about your products and all of their capabilities, as you speak about them your excitement should grow. You should be so excited and enthusiastic about your product or service that you practically can't contain it. This is the quality that is naturally embodied by the world's best sales professionals. They are passionate about what they do, and excited to share it with practically anyone who will listen. Key!

You Inc.

This advice applies to everyone, not just salespeople. See the company you work for in your own mind as if it is your own company. Behave as if you are responsible for every aspect of the company's success. Be on the lookout for ways to not only increase sales, but also to decrease expenses, improve efficiencies, and retain customers. Essentially, be committed to your company's total success.

Obviously, this includes areas that are outside the purview of your own expertise. For instance, one of the fastest ways to climb the company ladder is to identify the challenges your company may be facing and then endeavor to solve them. *Mindstorm* (focus on and list possible solutions) ways to solve these challenges until a solution presents itself. Also, connect with people who may have the answers or the resources to help eliminate these challenges. Then, once you identify the solutions, take them to the people in your company who have the ability or the authority to make them happen.

Don't be one of those people who say, "it's not my job." If you can influence something, then make it your job. Otherwise you may be standing by without a job as the collections company comes to take the office furniture away.

I believe that everyone in an organization is responsible for the company's total sales. If a company sells a product or service geared towards a broad spectrum of individual consumers and its employees are not inviting every one of their family and friends to purchase these items, they are failing as a member of that business. Regardless of how well the department does, or

22

how well they perform their responsibilities, if an employee is not doing all that he is capable of doing for that company, he should step aside and let someone takeover who will. The very best employed professionals assume the identity of company owner whether or not their job title reflects it, and they put that type of commitment into their work (and for salespeople this is even more important).

My wife takes this approach at her own job. At the dental office where she is employed, she has brought in countless friends and family members who have become patients (myself included). Everywhere she goes she is inviting people she meets to come into her dental office for a visit. She touts their level of service, the expertise of the dentists, and the programs they have to help kids and seniors alike with their own dental care.

She also has assumed the responsibility of ordering supplies for the office, and strives to be consistently decreasing expenses for her employer. Essentially, she treats their money as if it's her own.

In the back of the mind of every prospective customer is the concern over the level of service they will receive after the sale takes place. Will this salesperson still be there if the item they purchased stops working, or more services need to be delivered as part of the agreement? When you hold yourself to a high standard and conduct yourself as if you are the company owner, you dismiss the prospect's concerns, because they see their future business dealing embodied in your present conduct.

Outwork Them

When I was working on the sales floor at the car dealership, I would apply this concept of going the extra mile whenever I received what was called a "phone-up." A phone-up is when a random customer calls into the dealership to find out if we have a model in stock, or they are calling to get a price on a specific model. I noticed among my peers that whenever they would get a phone-up, they would simply answer the customer's question while asking the customer to commit to an appointment. Some prospective customers did, many did not.

I approached phone-ups differently. Whenever I got a phone-up, I would tell the customer in advance that not only would I confirm that the model is in stock, I would also get them a price on a cash buy, different payment options on a finance buy, two or three lease payment choices, as well as a list of the buying incentives and discounts available. Not only that, I'd be doing all of this, and then driving to their home or office to show them the car, basically saying "stay put, I am on my way."

As a result, I sold more phone-ups. I struck when the customer's excitement was high and they were motivated (at least motivated enough to call). If they weren't available to meet at that moment, I'd schedule the appointment at the dealership or their home, and then I'd send more information in advance of our appointment to help them to become even more excited. I did everything I could to surprise and impress them with my work ethic. My suggestion to you is to also do more than the customer requests and to surprise them further by delivering more than they could ever expect!

Summary:

In this chapter, we talked about getting in early, planning your day, and taking consistent action to "touch" people in meaningful ways. You can likely see how these strategies go well beyond selling. This applies to any job.

For example, let's say you are starting a new job where you lack experience, and find yourself at the bottom of the company ladder. The exciting news is you can make up for this lack of experience with concerted action. Your colleagues might think they are better positioned than you because they have been employed at the company longer. However, your commitment to action is at the very least an equalizer.

"The key to this philosophy is to see more prospective customers than your peers and the competition, and then to keep up this level of activity."

Warning: Sales Slump

There is an internal thermostat in all people that controls many of the effects that show up in their lives. For example, this internal thermostat not only controls how much money you make, but also how much you weigh, how well you perform, and how much effort and energy you expend on a regular basis. This thermostat is made up of your self-concept. Your self-concept is a combination of your internal self-image, your self-esteem, and your self-confidence. Your self-concept is not simply a product of your conscious mind, but is made up of your most deep seated beliefs.

This internal thermostat that you possess works the same as a thermostat in a person's home. For example, if in your home you have the thermostat set at seventy degrees and the temperature rises to seventy-two degrees, the thermostat will kick in and turn on the air conditioner which will bring the temperature back to the pre-determined setting.

This phenomenon works the same in our lives as well. For instance, if you have a specific weight that is a setting for you on your internal thermostat (often called a set-point), your subconscious mind, which influences your behavior, will keep you performing in a manner that maintains this set-point. For instance, if you lose a few pounds, your thermostat kicks in and you find yourself eating more and/or cutting back on exercise; thus the weight returns.

In your business, you currently have a pre-determined earnings thermostat that you may not have ever consciously decided upon. It is a result of unconscious beliefs and conditioning. When you hit the earnings set-point corresponding with the amount on your internal thermostat, you will find yourself pulling back your efforts often without even realizing it. Let's say that your money thermostat is set at earning $80,000 for the year and you achieve this by October. Instead, of driving your earnings up in November or December, you will find yourself missing out on sales, losing accounts, or having appointments chronically rescheduled. As a result, you don't sell anything for the next two months, and then things pick up again in January for you, when your thermostat kicks back on and aligns all your efforts.

25

The lack of sales in November and December represent a phenomenon which is commonly called a *sales slump.* The challenge is most people don't know why they're in a slump.

There are several ways to deal with this phenomenon. The first is to examine your beliefs to identify what earnings amount you have set your internal thermostat for. This can be challenging and take time because often the real amount is buried in your subconscious.

The second method seems to be less mentally taxing, and simply involves continually setting and moving towards higher goals. ***To prevent a slump you must keep raising the bar, and taking expanded actions consistent with hitting this new target.*** Often, this is the only way to change your thermostat in the short term.

Throughout this book, and especially in chapter five, we will focus on this key to controlling your internal thermostat; that is to keep setting challenging goals and regularly measuring your progress in relation to those goals.

This works because it is similar to building a muscle, learning a new skill, or even doing something very challenging like training for a marathon. When training for a marathon for example, you don't go out and try to run all 26.2 miles at once. Instead, you may start by running three miles and getting comfortable with this distance, and then when you are comfortable you expand it to five miles, and so on. As this pertains to money, most people maintain their earnings level by default. Instead, be constantly focused on expanding this number higher and higher.

Remember, be aware of this thermostat,
and keep moving the setting by expanding your goals.

Chapter Summary:

1. What you lack in skill you make up for in activity. Once you develop the skills through activity, don't slow down. Instead, keep up the activity and continue to increase it.
2. There is no down-time in sales. Your skills and rewards grow in proportion to your level of activity.
3. Repeat daily: "I do more than they could ever expect"
4. To operate at high volume in your activities you need to build systems. Systemize your entire approach. Develop a system for sending greeting cards, newsletters, and posting status updates on social media sites.
5. Develop the practice of planning your sales day the night before.
6. Before leaving the office at night, write your crucial six activities for the very next day.
7. Cultivate the philosophy of always striving to do more than the customer could ever expect.
8. Become a 24/7 professional in your thinking and actions.

Chapter Two

Key Concept #2

If you are not with a client, you had better be out getting clients.

In some sales roles the company will supply you with prospects. This is especially true if you work in a consumer sales company such as a bank, a store, or a dealership where customers walk in off the streets to seek out your offerings. Most salespeople in these roles think it's the responsibility of the company to continually supply them with prospective customers and leads. Equally, if you are not in a sales role, if you are in customer service, engineering, or production, you might think it's the company's job to bring in new clients as well. As mentioned briefly in the previous chapter, regardless of what type of role you have in the company, maintaining the perspective that it's the company's responsibility to keep the pipeline full can be very limiting to your own career and to the future of your company.

My father taught me a different way to look at this. He tried to teach this concept to all his salespeople but what he found was only the best are willing to do this. He said, "It is your responsibility to bring in customers. The value you bring to this dealership, frankly, the value you bring to any selling role or company you work for, is your personal network, those customers who come in specifically because of you and your sales and marketing. You need to be constantly cultivating your own network."

My father exemplified this concept. Previous customers spanning the last twenty years in which he had been in auto sales came in each week asking specifically for him. New customers that he would attract from the golf-course, at school functions for my brother and me, from our neighborhood, from restaurants he frequented, and of course from endless referrals, also came to see him regularly to buy a car.

My father taught me that the clients the company supplies, the ones who come in from company sponsored newspaper ads and TV commercials, those are the "icing on the cake." You cannot build a wildly successful business based on those customers. In most cases those are the same customers that everyone is vying for.

On the other hand, *Selling on the Extra Mile, means going out and building your own network and continually finding your own clients.* Fact in point, if you were to go online and read a job posting for an experienced salesperson, especially when a company is looking to hire someone to launch a new division or build a presence in a new sector, they are almost always looking for someone who already has an established network of customers in that area.

I believe it is everybody's responsibility in a company or business to be bringing in new customers. Lawyers and accountants who grow their own customer base in a firm become partners. The rest are relegated to the bottom rungs. Your network, the customers you cultivate through you own effort is the value you bring to your organization; and, is representative of your value to the marketplace. With a loyal customer base in your possession, you will never have to worry about being unemployed.

Regardless of your job title you must accept the responsibility of bringing new customers into your company. If you are in a sales role and aren't doing this, you are doing yourself and your company a major disservice. For instance, if you sell home appliances at Sears and everyone who knows you doesn't realize that they can buy a refrigerator, dishwasher, or stove from you, you are missing the opportunity to succeed. However, if everyone who knows you expects that you will be the source for their home appliance needs, then you will sell more. Plus, if you go a step further and develop strategic alliances with real estate agents and mortgage brokers for you both to refer customers to each other, then you will be exceptional. So make it your responsibility to fill your own pipeline even if the company does some of it for you.

Note: This concept builds on the previous one presented. In the first concept, you learned how to increase your activity to see more customers as well as to maximize the customers you currently had. This second concept will allow you to build on the first concept which is to see 3x the customers than everyone else, by going out and getting a lion's share of available prospects. So, as my father instilled in me, "If you are not with a client, you had better be out getting clients."

Next, I am now going to share with you the various effective strategies you can implement immediately to build your own customer base.

Be Known

You and your specific offering need to be known throughout your network and beyond. When someone thinks about the product or service you can offer, make sure they are thinking about you.

Choose to be visible; to be known in your local community and/or your business community. There are many ways to do this such as to write articles, leverage social media websites such as Facebook, Twitter or YouTube, sponsor local sports teams, host "Lunch and Learns," participate at fairs, develop strategic alliances, go to trade shows, do mailings, etc. All of these activities have one thing in common in addition to helping you to become known and visible. They all are geared towards building a constantly expanding network of prospective customers for you to sell to.

Networking

Prospecting for new customers and networking go hand in hand. When you network, network as you build your life. Don't make networking something separate that you solely do during business hours. This ties in to what I said before – successful people don't separate their business and their life (this why it is important to find something you love). People come to know them by their business. Think Donald Trump for example. He goes to work each day because he loves what he does and so he is constantly focused on it 24/7.

Networking Exercise:

The following is an exercise I created to help individuals to identify areas to expand their own network while being authentic and doing things that are relevant and interesting to them.

Here is how it works: What follows are the key areas of life as I view them. These areas are very important beyond selling to the realm of living a complete and full life. These areas include tending to your Spiritual nature, devoting time to your health and fitness, performing work that is impactful and meaningful, scheduling time to nurture those high value relationships, thinking about, planning and acting upon your financial goals, and, making a difference in society through your charitable endeavors.

The purpose of this exercise is to find ways to combine your business networking activities with your participation in these key areas, thus enabling you to live a full and rewarding life.

First, begin by identifying the key areas or components of your own life. For your convenience, beginning with the Spiritual component, I have listed the areas I think are most important:

Spiritual component: Do you devote a period of time each week to building a spiritual practice? Do you attend church, synagogue, mosque, temple, etc? If the answer is yes, then it is your goal to be certain that the members of your spiritual community know you and are aware of what you do, mainly the value your business can bring to the group.

For instance, if you make donations to your spiritual center such as a Tithe, be sure that the donations come through your business, even if you don't own the business. Likely, the business is probably where the bulk of your income comes from so when you share a piece of your income, give it as part of the business. An example of this approach might go like this: my tithing checks might be accompanied by a card that reads, *on behalf of Charles Householder of ABC Recruiting and Personnel.*

Next, get involved! Sponsor church events as an official representative of your company. Let everyone know, if they need the product or service your company sells, that they can get it from a trusted and liked fellow member of their spiritual community – which is you!

Take a moment now, and list some ways in which you can become more visible among the members of your spiritual community, or for the people who share your spiritual activities:

Bring a meal to the weekly potluck; place an Ad in the newsletter;

_____

_____

_____

_____

_____

_____

*By the end of this chapter you should have a substantial list of both potential contacts to reach out to, and networking activities to perform in order to become visible in your community.

Health and Fitness: How do you improve your health and fitness? Do you go to a gym, running club, yoga, or take a martial arts class?

The people who you exercise alongside of are either all potential customers or a possible leads to a potential company or business customer.

For instance, when I sold cars many of my own customers came from the gym. Back then, I would choose a nice new car and drive it to the gym when I intended to work out. I'd park it in front, and I'd let everyone know that they could buy that particular car from me.

I also sponsored events the gym was doing such as new member events. Later, when I sold insurance, I sponsored health programs at the gym where we would take blood pressure, measure height and weight, body mass index, and give health pamphlets. I would naturally present the fact that they could get various related insurance products from me. Of course, everyone who was even remotely interested received a free consultation.

What are some ways which you can promote your business and offering while tending to your health and fitness needs? Take a moment now and list them below:

_____

_____

_____

_____

_____

_____

_____

_____

Work/Vocation: Hopefully, you know I don't mean to sell your colleagues. Instead, what are some of the opportunities related to your work where you could attract new customers?   Trade organizations come to mind immediately.   In most of my professional selling roles I was always involved with at least one relevant trade organization. For instance, when I was in staffing sales, I was involved with the trade organizations that supported the industry for which my team recruited. Since we recruited scientists and engineers, I participated in technical organizations and the regular events they would conduct. Thereby, I would meet many of the hiring managers and decision makers who worked in the various companies I was targeting to assist. As a result, many of my clients came directly from the relationships I built by attending the functions hosted by these types of local organizations.

Years later when I began selling comprehensive PR and marketing programs, the industry I targeted was direct selling. The very first thing I did was to become involved with the Direct Selling Association. This relationship gave me immediate credibility and helped establish an affinity between my company and many of the DSA's members. We will discuss the importance of cultivating a perceived *affinity* as it pertains to influence in chapter six.

Another networking opportunity consistent with vocation is BNI. Business Networking International attracts professionals from all walks of life who realize the value of building their business through referrals and warm leads. BNI was founded on the concept of "Givers Gain." At BNI, your fellow members act like your own marketing team out telling your story and sharing the value you can bring. This organization is easy to join and presents a great opportunity to promote your business while helping others. Remember, people respond in kind. Help others promote their business and solve their challenges and they will help you.

Universal Axiom:
The more you give, the more you receive.

What are some of the trade organizations that support your industry which you can become a part of? For example, if you sell cars and are looking to increase fleet vehicle sales, perhaps joining a local trade organization for the construction industry would make sense.

Identify and list below the various trade organizations and professional associations which you can join.

Also, be sure to include networking groups such as BNI, as well as associations in and around your industry, and professional development groups/events as well. In fact, professional development events are one the best ways to network with the top professionals in a variety of fields.

---

*If you are having trouble identifying these types of organizations or groups, here are a few strategies to discover them:

1. Do a GOOGLE search to identify relevant trade organizations and associations.
2. Research what organizations your suppliers and/or competitors belong to.
3. Look for advertisements in relevant trade journals.
4. Ask members of your network.

Relationships: Just like with the work area, this doesn't mean just selling to family and friends. Although, many of your family members and friends should be clients if what you're offering is relevant. The point of this is to remind you how important it is that everyone in your family knows what you do and are encouraged to share you as a resource with their network.

For example, when I began selling cars I made sure that everyone I knew was aware that I too sold cars. This included all of my relatives, as well as my classmates from high school and college, and my friends.

Later, when I met my wife, I was actively employed selling life insurance. In addition to informing all of my own family and friends, I had her introduce me to all her family and friends as well. Since many of my wife's family were also from Colombia and some did not speak English, during appointments with them she would come along and translate. As a result, the trust they had in her naturally affected the way they chose to feel about me (shared affinity).

Six Degrees of Separation…from Kevin Bacon

Six degrees of separation (also referred to as the "Human Web") refers to the concept that everyone is on average approximately six people away from any other person on Earth. So by creating a chain linking a friend of a friend you can on average connect any two people in six steps or fewer.

I first was introduced to this idea when a friend shared with me the trivia game Six Degrees of Kevin Bacon. The game was based on the notion that the actor Kevin Bacon has basically worked with almost everyone in Hollywood and that any actor could be connected through this chain to Kevin Bacon with a few steps. For example, let's connect Elvis Presley to Kevin Bacon. Elvis Presley was in Change of Heart with Ed Asner in 1969. Ed Asner acted with Kevin Bacon in JFK in 1991. So Elvis is only 2 degrees from Kevin Bacon.

Six Degrees of Separation is a powerful concept which begs the question: *How many degrees are you away from the decision maker at any of the companies you would like to sell to?*

Who do you know that knows the CEO of a company at which you desire to sell? The key to using this networking skills exercise is by leveraging the people you know to gain an introduction to the person they know who is also a decision maker. Realize that you are likely just a few degrees from anyone you would want to sell to. Keep this in mind as you build your 100 list next, and maximize your network.

100 List

The 100 List is a very powerful networking technique which is very simple to do. In a moment, list 100 people you personally know and have some sort of relationship with. These people can be called your *natural market*. These are people you know that also know you, and would likely return the phone call if you left them a message. To maximize your 100 List perform the following three steps.

1. Below, write a list of 100 people you know well (use additional paper).
2. Reach out to all of them making sure they are aware of your offering.
3. Ask for an appointment or a referral to a prospective customer (see how to ask for referrals at the end of this chapter).

Money: One of the ways to apply networking in relation to your money is to use the following technique called:

I.   *Create your own Financial Board of Directors*

It is my belief that everyone, regardless of income, should have a specific lawyer, accountant, real estate agent, insurance agent, and mortgage broker on call that they do business with.

Since these professionals also rely on networking and referrals to build their business, you can cultivate a relationship with each financial professional by sending them referrals, and usually they will respond in kind.

Another method for networking as it pertains to the category of money is called:

II.   *Follow your Dollar*

Here is how it works: Identify where you spend your money, and include those vendors in your marketing plans. Reach out to them by phone or in person to make sure they know what you do. Create strategic alliances with them if appropriate, and always, ask for referrals.

Take a moment now to list potential individuals who can make up your own **Financial Board of Directors**. Once you've done that, list appropriate vendors, specifically places where you or your company spends money (**Follow you Dollar**). These individuals will represent great sources to contact for networking and gaining new customers.

_____

_____

_____

_____

_____

_____

Community and Charity: A great way to meet influential people from all walks of life and to make a difference is through charity. Non-profit organizations such as the United Way, YMCA, Boys and Girls Club, and other charitable organizations present great choices.

In my own life, when I volunteered for Dress for Success (DFS) I was subsequently introduced to the Board of Directors for DFS who I then followed up with to cultivate a relationship. Since the board was made up of c-level decision makers from many of the top companies in Connecticut, I soon gained an easy entrée to all those companies to present my products and services.

To network in this area, begin by identifying a *cause* near and dear to your heart, and then look for ways to get involved. Once you have identified the particular causes and corresponding charities you are going to support, do get involved. Go to their events. Participate in fundraisers. Join their board of directors. Meet outside of the charity with other like-minded members. Use these meetings as an opportunity to cultivate a business relationship as well.

Invest some time in the immediate future to identify a charitable organization with which to partner. To get you started, take a moment and list several causes that come to mind which you would like to support.

Note: The major theme of this exercise is to prepare you to inform everyone you know and continue to meet, what you do and how you can help them. Pay attention to where you are spending your time, and who you are associating with. Then purposefully cultivate your network in each of these areas.

Summary: At this point you now have a working list of networking opportunities and people to reach out to in order to grow your business. Apply the related strategies contained in this book in order to continually cultivate this network.

The following are additional strategies for ATTRACTING more customers:

Give the Impression of Success

People want to do business with successful people. Successful people characteristically hold themselves to a higher standard. They strive to deliver top-notch products and services. Additionally, they are *connectors*. Since successful people typically do business with other successful people, they have the ability to *connect* different people for the purpose of conducting mutual business. Often, as a rule, the most successful people are quick to refer other successful individuals they meet to the people in their own network. As a result, by cultivating relationships with successful people you can gain access to their network as well.

To give the impression of success, you must live successfully. I have discovered that the best salespeople predictably live the best lives. By "best" I am referring to quality. They go to the best events, eat at the best restaurants, attend the best shows, and know all the best people. They are a total embodiment of living a life of success and as a result they attract other successful people to them very easily. This attractive quality must never be overlooked as it pertains to developing more and more business. You wear your lifestyle on you like a suit. It shows up in how you speak, how you carry yourself, and of course how you spend your time. With this in mind, endeavor to raise your standards in order to enhance your lifestyle. Discover what's fun and exciting and incorporate those activities into your life. Of course, always choose quality over quantity.

To give the impression of success in your business you must choose to go beyond solving challenges by making sure your product or service can enhance the life of you customer. Seek to help the prospective customer

40

enjoy their present and prepare for their future. You accomplish this by painting a picture in their mind of future success by doing business with you. Give them the feeling that through the product or service they gain by doing business with you they will experience their own success. Once you've painted that picture, you then do everything you can to help that picture be realized.

*In Chapters seven and eight of this book, you will learn specifically how to present your offering in a way that goes far beyond just solving problems.

Set Up Strategic Alliances

Partner with other business professionals who sell different products than you, but sell them to the same types of customers. For example, by setting up strategic alliances with real estate and insurance agents who were all vying for the same customers, is how I grew the mortgage company I managed.

A mortgage sale is multi-faceted and involves attorneys, real estate agents, appraisers, inspectors, movers, insurance agents, etc. The list is lengthy. As a result, I would be constantly building strategic alliances with these types of professionals and recommending them to all of my own customers. They in turn would refer their customers and help me to promote my business as well.

You can also develop a strategic alliance with a business in an entirely different industry. For example, when I was selling insurance, our company relocated to a new office park. In the office park was a corporate gym that many of us purchased membership at in order to exercise during early mornings or late evenings. By the way, the gym proved to be a great place to meet other executives who also became clients. One afternoon, my colleague went into the gym to enroll himself and saw a flyer for the on-site child daycare company's upcoming open house. He grabbed the flyer and gave it to me suggesting I speak to the Director of the daycare company about us participating at the open house. I immediately contacted the person in charge, and she happily agreed to have us at her event. I arrived early one

Saturday morning, and set up a vendor table to speak to parents about college planning, life insurance, and other options to protect and provide for their families. My participation at the event was a hit and I attracted many new clients. I then reached out to that particular daycare franchise's other locations looking to partner with all of them. As a result, on several Saturdays during two distinct times of year, I would host my own table at the various open houses, and at other events at the daycare as potential clients lined up to speak with me. The best part was, I was the only one from my industry doing this, making this captive audience practically mine!

80/20 Rule

The Pareto principle, which is also commonly known as the 80/20 rule, is named after Italian economist Vilfredo Pareto who developed the concept from observation of Italy's distribution of real estate. He discovered that 80% of Italy's land was owned by 20% of the population. Later, it was discovered that the 80/20 rule can be used to make accurate observations about many distinct occurrences.

Following along with this principle, in sales you will find that 20% of your efforts make up 80% of your results. 20% of your clients make up 80% of your total sales revenue. The key then to leveraging this knowledge is to identify what types of clients make up your top 20%, and to focus on finding more like them.

A few years ago, I was hired to consult for a nutrition company with a great product but stagnant sales. The first thing I decided to do was to review their books to identify the types of customers they were selling to and how the sales force was marketing to these customers. I discovered that the sales team was spending the majority of their time calling small "mom and pop" nutrition store owners who made up 80% of the total customer list, but combined accounted for roughly 20% of their revenue. On the other hand, the smaller amount of large customers who made up 80% in revenue were not given as much focus. For example, in the group that made up 80% of top revenue were international sales distributors. However, this nutrition company was only working with 2-3 of these distributors. From this

42

discovery, I immediately directed the sales team to begin focusing on attracting additional international distributors and retailers. As a result, with each new international retailer who signed on the nutrition company was able to easily increase sales significantly.

Do this exercise at your company by analyzing your own sales data now. Identify where your customers come from – who are your top 20%? What do they have in common? Where can you find more of the higher revenue producing clients?

For example, if you owned a local dance school, you could do a survey of all of your students and determine what commonalties they share. Do they come from the same town? Are they in the same clubs or school programs? Do they or their parents work at the same companies? With this information, you can then specifically target those areas with your marketing and sales to gain more customers.

Everyone is in Sales

When I was in college I launched my own martial arts school inside a local YMCA facility. Initially, I imagined that the majority of my time would be spent teaching and practicing the martial arts. However, I soon discovered that a vast majority of my time needed to be spent attracting students. Analyzing this, I came to the conclusion that I wasn't just a martial arts instructor, I was really a *sales and marketing professional* in the role of martial arts instructor. Once I made this distinction, my enrollment skyrocketed!

The success of your business will be determined by how well you can sell and market yourself. If you are a salesperson you must accept that you are really a sales and marketing professional in the role of sales. I know I used the word *sales* twice, so let me make it more clear. If you sell copiers, then in actuality you are a sales and marketing professional in the role of copier salesperson. Your first responsibility then is to market yourself and your business in order to gain selling appointments to present your product, which in this example is copiers.

If you think that in your professional role you are the furthest from sales, perhaps for an example, you are an electrical engineer, I would respond by suggesting you go back to the previous chapter where I share with you the concept that to be truly successful in business and in life you must see yourself as "You Inc." As You Inc., it is your job to market and sell yourself to potential employers and customers.

Key: The same is true for you in your business as well, especially if you are in sales. You are a sales and marketing professional in the role of _____.

Go Beyond the Competition

This suggestion is easy. If you want to go beyond what the competition would do, give value without the guarantee of getting something in return. The vast majority of organizations, small through large, live by the philosophy that they will provide value once they get paid. In Selling on the Extra Mile you are encouraged to give value up front, and to give value without guarantees. Like the Seeder in the parable in the Bible, spread your seeds far and wide.

Also, just like in the example of the wood stove which can only heat the home once the wood is put in it. It's not the other way around, you can't say to the stove, "heat the house, and then I will put wood in you." You must put the wood in first. Likewise, you give value first and then you enjoy the just returns.

Give value even without the guarantee
of getting something back in return.

I came to this conclusion naturally when teaching martial arts as a young man. Because I loved practicing the martial arts so much, I enjoyed teaching extra classes, hosting public seminars, or putting on large scale events. In fact, two of these things in particular dramatically increased enrollment in my programs.

The first was an idea I had one day while driving to college. While driving through an impoverished area and seeing children standing on corners and hanging around in the streets, I had the idea that martial arts could help develop positive character attributes in these kids. Realizing that it was likely their parents might not be able to afford martial arts lessons, I decided to volunteer and teach a free class that focused on life skills in addition to the martial arts. Well, word of this class spread like wildfire and I was featured in the local newspaper and talked about throughout the community. As a result I attracted many more students to all my classes.

The next idea was in response to a challenge my martial arts mentor Tom was going through. His granddaughter had been born with a rare brain disorder and he was looking for ways to raise money for medical organizations researching possible treatments. This spawned the idea for me to hold a charity martial arts tournament to raise money to support his cause. Again, the newspapers and word of mouth spread the news and following the tournament class enrollment quadrupled. Later on what I discovered was that no other schools really hosted their own large scale tournaments. This was generally done by professional organizations that catered to martial artists. Since mine was geared towards spectators and their enjoyment, attendance went through the roof.

Furthermore, back then when I was doing these events, there wasn't any social media to help publicize them. In today's day and age, providing value for free to the masses can be publicized through social media providing access to an audience of unlimited proportions.

Make this strategy work for your organization. Think of ways you can provide value up-front in your industry or community. Examples might be through blog articles, newsletters, events, or sponsorships. It's alright if your offering is free in the beginning, because eventually this approach will pay dividends.

Be High Tech and High Touch

I know I keep harping on about social media, however, as it pertains to this chapter, it is vital to realize that social media allows you to go from being perceived as a hunter to that of a fisherman. Since customers in general do not want to be hunted, by providing interesting and informative content to your social following, you make yourself *attractive bait.*

Begin immediately to implement the following into your business:

1. Create a Facebook Fan Page for your business and invite all of your family, friends, colleagues, and customers to join.
2. Create a LinkedIn profile and join professional groups on LinkedIn.
3. Post frequent updates on Facebook and LinkedIn to keep your followers engaged. Use Twitter which can link to multiple sites at once.
4. Create a regular newsletter showcasing your products or services. Run contests among your customers. Use a free service such as Mail Chimp to manage your newsletter and list.
5. Create relevant videos using a video camera, or the video camera on your smart phone. Host them on YouTube and post them on your Facebook page.

This is just the tip of the iceberg in terms of how you can leverage social media to promote your business. If you are not taking advantage of at least the five preceding things you are missing out. Implement them now and be on the lookout for different ways to engage your followers.

Referrals

If you have a thriving referral business you won't have to do as much canvassing and cold calling. In addition, everyone knows that referrals as a rule have a very high likelihood of becoming a sale. If you desire to go from closing one or two out of ten, to closing eight out of ten, referrals is the vehicle to do just that. What follows are two of the best ways to get referrals for your business:

The first method is to...drum roll please...ASK. The best salespeople who I have studied that are known to consistently get referrals do so because they always ASK.

You may be thinking, "I also ask, but seldom get referrals, how can this be the case?" The key to getting referrals is sometimes determined by how you ask. When asking, don't be too general. Narrow your request down. For instance, when at the car dealership, I would ask questions that were related to the buying patterns of my target market. For example, I would ask the question, "Who do you know that started a new job?" The reason I asked this question is because I had found that people who started a new job, or were promoted to a better position often bought new cars shortly thereafter.

Another question was, "Who do you know that just had kids, or are about to have kids?" Again, the reason for this question was because I had recognized that the people who were about to have children, usually bought larger family oriented vehicles.

To recap, the two keys are:

1. Ask narrow questions. Make it so they don't have to search their entire mind thinking of people they know. Narrow it down for them by asking for specific types of people.
2. Realize that life changes precipitate buying changes. Life changes such as graduating from school, getting a new job, getting married, having a child, all necessitate new buying patterns.

The previous example related to selling a consumer sales product. The fact is that in business sales it really doesn't change. For instance, at trade organizations, decision makers from many companies throughout an entire industry are all getting together. As a result executives from competing companies will meet regularly, be on trade organization committees or boards, and interact in other ways. So if you are speaking to one executive,

47

he or she can connect you to many of their peers, just through the relationships contained in the trade organization in which they belong.

When asking executives for a referral always use the same format which is to begin by asking narrow questions. Questions such as, do you belong to any boards? Who else is on there? What companies did you work at before? Who do you know from those specific companies?

Once you identify a potential referral, ask the person who is providing the referral to contact them now. Extra Mile salespeople never wait to act.

Bonus: Referrals on the Extra Mile

The next question I am often asked about getting referrals is, "when should I ask for a referral?"

The answer is, once you've earned the right to ask.

There are two ways in which you can earn the right to ask for a referral. The first is to do an amazing job at fulfilling the present client's need, and then allow them the privilege of passing on the same benefits to their friends and family.

The second way to earn the right to ask for a referral is to give referrals. At BNI there is a back and forth giving of referrals by people who know each other, but may have never experienced the product or service the other is offering. So why do they give this person whom they have never bought from an endless flow of referrals? The primary answer is simply because the other person is continually giving them referrals.

Whenever possible, be sure to give referrals to your customers. Send business their way. Turn them into friends and partners by helping them to succeed. As Zig Ziglar, the famous motivational speaker has said, "you can get in life anything you want by helping enough people get what they want." Giving referrals and sharing customer leads is how you help them to get what they want.

Go the extra mile in getting referrals by doing something very few salespeople do, and that is give referrals. Be a connector, by keeping your own network top of mind, and always be looking for ways to connect people who can help each other.

Chapter Summary:

1. If you are not with a client, you had better be out getting clients. There is no downtime in sales or success.
2. It is everyone in the company's responsibility to attract new customers.
3. A major value experienced salespeople bring to their work is their existing network of potential customers.
4. You must constantly be cultivating your network and building your pipeline.
5. Position yourself favorably in your community through events and social media.
6. Become known and get connected to as many viable prospects as possible by combining technology with your other activities.
7. Network as you build your life. People buy from people like themselves, and the best place to find people like you is where you enjoy to hang out.
8. People want to do business with successful people. Be sure people perceive you as a success.
9. Partner with people who sell different products and services than you do, but sell to the same people.
10. Know where your best customers come from, and focus 80% of your efforts there.
11. The best way to get referrals is to give referrals.

Chapter Three

Key Concept #3

What you initially lack in skill you must make up for in persistence.

Statistics show that the average sale happens on the 5ᵗʰ call. I have found this to be anything but average. The fact is that most salespeople hardly ever make it that far. They give up on the prospective client at the first "no" or potential roadblock. Successful salespeople on the other hand persist by keeping the proverbial ball moving down the field until a sale is made.

My father shared with me the following strategy when I began selling cars. He said that there was a paradox to a customer's behavior. Initially, potential customers usually don't want to be hunted. They would prefer to decide in advance where to shop based on whose marketing, advertising, and offers appeared to be the most attractive, or who they specifically knew(this is key). However, once they entered the water, so to speak, they wanted to be pursued.

Unfortunately, this is where most salespeople fail. Often, the average salesperson will go through their presentation, perhaps do a competent needs analysis, present options, and maybe go ahead and ask for the business. However, there are a variety of factors that can often be overlooked and unaccounted for by the average salesperson during the presentation (Those who sell on the extra mile shorten the sales cycle by learning many new techniques and strategies such as those presented in this book). As a result, the buying decision is put off until a later date. At this point, the average salesperson typically pulls back and eventually loses out to a more persistent professional.

My father recognized this phenomenon and shared with me the following words to help guide my approach to dealing with customers. He said, "What you initially lack in skill you must make up for in persistence. Persistence has a magical quality which influences the buyer. They want to be pursued. They want to know that their business matters. When you commit to a high level of persistence you will succeed regardless of what close you use."

Over the years, I have cultivated this quality of persistence and applied it to all aspects of my selling including my networking and prospecting activities. In addition, I have valued every single customer I have had the privilege of presenting to, and even though my skills have improved dramatically and I am now able to qualify a customer and help them reach a buying decision quicker and easier, I still continue to practice persistence as a rule.

In this chapter, you will discover how to position yourself as a committed and persistent professional without becoming an annoyance.

Just as with the first lesson, even after your skills increase, your level of activity and in this case, persistence, must never diminish.

Persistence (Stalk, Obsess, Relentless)

The approach the best salespeople take when selling would get them locked up in the everyday world. For example, I have been known to **stalk** a potential client by first researching them intently via the internet. Next, I have extended my intelligence gathering to include questioning other people they do business with. Finally, I will often call them until I get an appointment or a definitive reason why I should call on someone else instead. As part of my telephone strategy, I will implement a coordinated marketing campaign that may include letters, post cards, sample products, and other correspondence.

Once I get the appointment, I will devote all my energy to the point of **obsess**ion in helping them to pinpoint their needs and to make the connection to how my product or service can satisfy those needs and solve their challenges.

Even if the customer doesn't buy during the first meeting, if we have established that my solution is what they need, I am then **relentless** in my pursuit of implementing the solution. I will assume a "whatever it takes" mentality; thinking about and focusing on the client as well as taking actions in the form of follow-up calls, emails, correspondence, etc. Like the best salespeople, I will only stop my persistent approach when the customer implements or presents a *"valid no"*.

So what is a *valid no*? A *valid no* can occur at any time in the process. It's when <u>you and the customer</u> come to the shared conclusion that there isn't a need for your product. Perhaps if you are selling speedboats in the middle of the Sahara Desert, many customers may present a *valid no* very early on in the process.

Remember, putting in persistent effort in reaching out to potential customers, and persisting in helping them make buying decisions, is how you demonstrate by your actions how much you value their business. You avoid annoying them by respecting a *valid no* and always have a business reason when reaching out to them.

What follows are some of the best, selling strategies consistent with the concept of persistence which I have discovered and applied:

Lay the Foundation to Practice Persistence

Time breeds familiarity and familiarity leads to trust. This concept recognizes the underlying axiom that people buy from people they like and trust. This is true, was true, and will always be true. Only in extremely rare instances or desperate situations, will somebody invest money in a product or service being sold by someone they neither like nor trust. If you don't already know your potential customer, it takes time for them to develop a basic liking and trusting of you. The more time you spend with the customer demonstrating your level of integrity and professionalism, the more comfortable they will become with buying from you. This level of comfort is what motivates them to share with you all of their concerns or complaints (normally called **objections**) allowing you to remedy them.

At the auto dealership, it was common among the other salespeople to want to rush through the sales presentation to get to the negotiation. These salespeople believed that price was the most important factor. As a result they spent too little time with the customer, failing to give them exceptional service, and failing to gain their trust. These people would sell only on price, and when you only sell on price, you almost always lose even when you make the sale.

One of the ways in which you transition from being viewed as a transactional salesperson who purely sells on price, to more of a trusted advisor who presents value and solves challenges, is by practicing behaviors consistent with this concept of *time leads to trust*. The more time you spend with the customer, the more you learn about their needs, interests, likes, and current situation, the more poised you are to make recommendations, and the more likely they are to act on them. So the key is to invest the necessary time to serve the prospect well. Also, master and apply the strategies in this book and your time will pay dividends to you.

Always Have a New Reason to Call

This is the way to separate persistence from annoyance. When I sold cars, I was told to keep in regular contact with my prospective customers. Initially, I would do this by just picking up the phone and calling to say hello, and then I would ask a stupid question, such as "so did you buy a car yet?" Often, the call would end with no new next steps. Eventually I got wiser, and decided I would only call customers when I had something specifically new to call and tell them. The funny thing was, each time I called them with new information I found them to be pleased rather than annoyed.

The good news is, there are always plenty of new reasons to call, **IF** you are immersed in your industry. To immerse yourself, begin now by subscribing to related trade journals and newsletters from vendors, manufacturers, and organizations that support your industry. In fact, have your fingers on the pulse of the industry. Be aware of and constantly chronicling new reasons to call. Then reach out to your customers in a variety of fashions such as telephone, email, and regular mail in the form of postcards, letters, and flyers. Keep high touch and be persistent. Never find yourself in a position where your customer tells you about something happening in your industry that you weren't aware of. Be on top of the happenings related to your product or service including incentives, what your competitors are doing, news headlines related to what you offer, etc.

Note: All of the strategies presented in this book are designed to tie nicely together. For instance, by immersing yourself in your industry you not only become more skilled, but you place yourself in a position to perform more networking.

Have a Lucky 20 List

There is no better profession in which you are positioned to create your own good luck than in selling. Luck has often been defined as when preparation meets opportunity. Part of preparation is focus. By focusing intently on a customer and their needs, you keep them top of mind. By keeping them top of mind you engage your *reticular activating system*. The reticular

55

activating system is part of the reticular cortex in your brain that has the ability to filter information in your environment and then bring into your conscious awareness similar information related to the subject of your focus. For instance, by focusing on your customers regularly, your reticular cortex is able to identify from your environment relevant resources to help you to make a sale with them.

For example, when I was working in PR sales, one of my target customers was The Pampered Chef. I very badly wanted to add them to our client list for a variety of reasons. The first reason was that from what I knew about them, I felt our program could have measurable positive impact on their business and bottom line. The second reason is I wanted my company to enjoy the prestige of having as a client one of the leaders in the direct selling industry. So I kept them on a sheet of paper called my "Lucky 20 List" which listed my top 20 ideal customers (who at that time may not have even ever been contacted). I would keep this list on my person and would refer to this list several times throughout the day.

One day I was in the Barnes and Noble bookstore and saw a book by the founder of the Pampered Chef, Doris Christopher, in which she gave a biographical depiction of how she created the company, and chronicled its growth to almost the present day. Had the Pampered Chef not been on my list I may have overlooked the book. This time I did not and with the information it contained I was able to build a case for how we could bring value to this company. This information had an immediate effect on my prospecting calls, and within a week I had an appointment. Coincidently, while flying out to Chicago on my way to this appointment, I was reading this book, and discovered that the woman sitting next to me was one of their top distributors and was on her way to a meeting that would include the top brass. Talk about the power of the Law of Attraction in action! I gave her my pitch and she loved it. She also provided me with much more information than was available in the book. As a result I was able to move the Pampered Chef from my Lucky 20 List to our actual client roster.

Apply this strategy immediately in your own business. Write a list of your potential and prospective customers. Include the company name, the

56

decision maker, and the ideal next step. Have your list with you at all times and refer to it often throughout the day. Visualize yourself frequently selling to these companies even if your visualizations at first are just pure un-abased fantasy.

Next, use your list as a prospecting tool. For example, when I sold autos I identified what companies in my community bought fleet vehicles and I put them on my list. Then I would ask everyone I spoke to if they knew anyone who worked at these companies. When they knew someone at the intended company, I would ask if I could use them as a reference to this person. Next, I'd make the call and gain permission to present our dealership as a viable resource for their next fleet order. Finally, I would make it my *written goal* to sell them multiple vehicles at any one time. That is it! Remember, what you focus on and think about you bring about, which is why you always keep your list nearby (as a focus tool).

My Lucky Twenty List (sample)

1. ABC COMPANY, John Doe, VP Communications, schedule mtg.

2. _____

3. _____

. _____

. _____

. _____

. _____

. _____

. _____

. _____

. _____

. _____

. _____

20. _____

Implement Focus Days

This is one of my favorite strategies for the Extra Mile salesperson. This approach allows the sales professional to be completely focused in such a way that they position themselves to marshal all of their creative resources to be applied to persistent selling.

Here is how it works:

Begin by dividing the various days of the week into either **Selling Days, Administrative/Service Days,** and **Marketing/Advertising Days**. Also, include a **Free day** each week, or so as appropriate.

Whereas the average salesperson will try to do a little selling, marketing, administrative paperwork, and client retention all on the same day, never getting as much done as they could if their days were completely focused, The Extra Mile professional will set up specific days for each type of activity and will focus single-mindedly on performing tasks consistent with the theme for that particular day.

Here is an example of how this works: Since most salespeople on average don't have Service Days, they deal with clients only when the client has a problem. By having a regular Service Day and reaching out to all your clients on that day, your clients don't have problems because you are essentially high touch. Also, Service Days typically become referral days as you discover from the regular attention you are giving your clients, that their problems diminish and their appreciation flourishes.

The key is to divide up your days and then perform the appropriate actions on the corresponding day. For example, do your intelligence gathering, work on flyers and sell sheets, as well as advertisements, social media and other forms of marketing on your Marketing Days.

On your selling days be totally focused and in the selling zone. Have scheduled as many sales appointments as possible with potential customers. If you don't have specific appointments scheduled, use these selling days to prospect, and follow-up with your previous and current customers for potential upsells. Apply persistent selling as a rule and continue to find new ways to move the proverbial ball down the field.

On your Service Days call all of your customers to ensure their satisfaction. Answer any questions they may have, tell them about new features and options coming available in the future. You will discover that it is on Service Days in which you will often get new referrals, and schedule new appointments to sell additional services.

On Free days, leave the smart phone at home, and disengage from work. Use this time to refresh. However, if an opportunity crosses your path, don't let it lie there too long. Remember, you are a 24/7 professional.

Chapter Summary:

1. A hallmark of all successful salespeople is their willingness to persist in making the sale.
2. Most sales take an average of five sales calls. Most salespeople give up after the first.
3. What you initially lack in skill you must make up for in persistence.
4. Once your skills increase, your level of persistence does not decrease.
5. Time breeds familiarity, and familiarity breeds trust. Since people buy from people they like and trust, commit the time to know your client.
6. Research prospective customers thoroughly via the internet.
7. Always have a new reason to call. Never call just to "check in."
8. Invoke the power of Focus and the Law of Attraction by leveraging a "Lucky 20" list.
9. Implement specific "focus days."
10. On your selling days, sell. Start early, and finish late, but conduct as many quality appointments as possible. On your administrative days, do all the paperwork. Don't divide your focus.

Chapter Four

Key Concept #4

The 80-15-5 Ratio.

I started selling cars in August, and was told by my colleagues that it was going to be slow around the holidays. In fact, I came to discover, that this was a commonly held belief among many salespeople. My father on the other hand said to me one afternoon that this is total bull and then he shared with me the *80-15-5 ratio.*

The *80-15-5 ratio* says that 80% of your success is based on intangibles such as discipline, persistence, energy, and attitude; and, 15% is based on sales techniques and skill in delivering them. He also expressed that a positive sincere attitude often makes up for a lack of skill (which is why new salespeople usually start off fast). Lastly, only 5% of your success would be based on the economy, perceived season, market, or even the particular product.

What I soon realized is that the reason many salespeople fail is because they change the ratio. The average salesperson often comes to believe, demonstrated by things they say and do, that 95% of his success is based on things outside of his control such as the economy. This clearly is not accurate.

For the Extra Mile salesperson the truth inherent in the 80-15-5 ratio is empowering because we can control the 95% - our psychology, persistence, attitude, and our skills. Plus, we can consciously go to work on improving each of the aforementioned, expanding our capacity, thereby improving our results.

The 80%:

Let's begin by talking about the 80% which is a part you can actually control. This part has a lot to do with your psychology. In sales, the components of your psychology, such as your attitude and self image, along with how you express your psychology by your behaviors, is crucial to your success.

Positive Attitude

Fact: Regardless of what's going on, people want to do business with positive people. Even negative thinking people don't often want to be around negative salespeople. Since a positive attitude is often the outward manifestation of a variety of other qualities such as enthusiasm, energy, and focus, by developing and reinforcing your own positive attitude, these attributes expand as well.

Having a positive attitude is not something nice to have, it's an absolute must. Like the flu, attitudes are contagious. Unlike the flu, people want to be caught up (catch) with another person's positive mental attitude (PMA).

Napoleon Hill, bestselling author of Think and Grow Rich said, "the human brain is a transmitter...and people pick up on your attitude telepathically." This means that your PMA has an influencing effect that can telepathically influence the buying proclivity of your prospective customer.

The key then is to work on improving and maintaining your positive attitude every single day. You can begin to do this simply by smiling, thinking positive and expansive thoughts, and when presented with problems choosing to focus on possible solutions.

Another factor that has an almost immediate effect on improving attitude is movement. Psychologists have long realized that a person's physiology affects their attitude. For example, you can't hold a smile for long without feeling better. Plus, if you are feeling tired, a little movement such as exercise or dance can go a long way in helping you to feel better.

Vocabulary is another factor that contributes to attitude. However, vocabulary also plays two distinct roles in this philosophy of selling. The first use of vocabulary is in choosing the words you use to communicate with yourself. Ensuring that your words are geared in a positive direction has a powerful effect on how you feel and how well you perform on the job.

Begin by paying attention to your vocabulary. Avoid words that dramatize problems or other negative effects that might occur. For instance, eliminate the word *problem* from your vocabulary and replace it with the word *challenge*. Choose to talk mainly about solutions. Eliminate the word *cost* and replace it with *investment*. People don't want to know how much something is going to cost them, but are more inclined to feel good about an investment they are making. Eliminate negatives and words that discount, such as *shouldn't, can't, not only, never mind*, etc. Replace with *how well, much*, and *in addition too*.

When people ask you how you feel, respond by saying words such as *great, fantastic*, or *terrific*. Say this enough throughout the day and you just might convince yourself. Focus on possibilities and things that you "can" do, and don't speak of limitations. Lastly, never condemn, criticize, or gossip about another person. This says more about you than it does about them anyway.

When selling, use gradient words that grow in a positive direction. Take a look at the following statements noticing how each phrase is designed to influence the answer in a positive direction:

How well do you like it?
How much better is this?
What more would you like?
How much sooner?
How wonderful would this be?

Another way to manufacture a positive attitude especially when faced with temporary challenges (yours or the prospect's), is by choosing to focus on the solution. Often, just by choosing to focus on the solution, you affect your behavior in a way that ultimately engineers a positive result. So begin the practice of solution thinking today. In fact, solution thinking should be the all pervading mindset of all salespeople in their own lives and in the lives of their prospective customers.

In the marketplace, you are not selling a product or service, you are selling a solution. Your solution should be solving many challenges in the prospective customers business and/or life. It's really pretty simple: they present the problem, you present the solution.

As a sales professional, the language that I choose to speak is its own language akin to sales filled with positivity and optimism!

The next ingredient contained in cultivating a positive mental attitude is enthusiasm. Enthusiasm has an energy all its own. People make buying decisions with their mind and heart. Usually, their heart first, and the mind second. Your enthusiasm speaks directly to their heart. If you can't be enthusiastic you can't really sell.

It's because of enthusiasm that I was a fantastic used car salesperson. I realize there is a stigma attached to the role of used car salesperson, but there shouldn't be. Like my peers, I was a fantastic used car salesperson because I wasn't trying to fool anyone, or trick them. The reason I was performed well is because I was totally enthusiastic about our inventory of pre-owned cars. The reason for this can easily be traced back to my teenage years. When I got my driver's license, I hadn't saved up much money for a car. As a result, my first car was a fifteen year old dilapidated American Motors Concord. I drove it for a year, happy to have a car, but wishing it was something better. Fortunately, I was able to sell it the following year for a profit. Eventually, when I began selling cars and saw the quality of used cars we had in inventory, I fell in love with each of them. Every time I would show a customer a used car, I would be brimming with positivity and enthusiasm. Often, their energy would rise to match mine. We would sync up!

In my experience with used-car customers, I found out that although some purchased used cars for the financial benefit such as the ability to avoid paying for the initial depreciation of a new car, the majority of customers bought used because they couldn't afford a new one. As a result, they would enter the dealership already feeling a little disappointed, but then they would meet me and I would be so excited about the cars I was showing them that my excitement and enthusiasm was contagious. This went a long way in my being able to influence the buyer (key).

To become enthusiastic, simply act enthusiastic.

Energy

In addition to attitude, energy is a vital component which makes up the 80% of your success. Selling on the Extra Mile requires energy, and lots of it. It takes massive energy to operate at a higher level than your peers. How do you raise your energy? Richard Branson, the billionaire owner of the Virgin group, was once entertaining a group of business professionals on his boat off the island he owns, and the question came up about how he was able to successfully create and lead upwards of the three hundred companies that make up Virgin. In other words, where did he get the time and energy? Everyone waited with bated breath for his answer. He was able to summarize the answer to this key to his success in one word, "exercise."

Our bodies and minds are adaptive, and our capacity expands each time we push ourselves to perform more. For example, start waking up each day an hour early, and within 21-30 days your body will have adapted to the change. By the way, just think what one more hour a day can do for your business.

Getting back to exercise and how it increases energy; countless studies have demonstrated that people who are in the best shape physically, essentially are most fit, naturally enjoy the most energy.

To increase your energy, commit to consuming a healthy diet. Avoid sugary processed foods. Stay away from high fat, fast foods. Choose to fast for a meal, instead of consuming fast foods. Eat highly nutritious foods such as fruits and vegetables in small portions throughout the day. *For more information on cultivating a healthy fit lifestyle refer to chapter eight in my book Warrior of Life: A Guide to Self-Transformation.

Summary: Sales is holistic. If you aren't disciplined, it will affect your sales. Be disciplined in your lifestyle and your commitment to harnessing more energy. For instance, get sufficient sleep. Rise the same time each day. Plan your meals in advance, and don't forget to plan your sales day the night before! These disciplines will help you gain momentum and will transfer to all the other important areas of your life.

Law of Attraction

The Law of Attraction is fully active in the world of selling. The Law of Attraction states that you attract people and circumstances to you based on your most dominant thoughts. Since our thinking is part of the 80% which we can control, directing our thoughts in a positive manner goes a long way in attracting to us positive results.

To make use of the Law of Attraction and to apply it to your business, do the following on a daily basis:

1. Think positive thoughts consistent with your goals.
2. Arrive early and visualize your sales appointments. See the sale complete in your mind's eye.
3. Affirm what you want to be true. Repeat audible affirmations such as "something good is going to happen to me today."
4. Take the actions suggested throughout this book such as keeping a Lucky 20 List.

The 15%:

The 15% of the ratio pertains to knowledge and skill. Even though sales specific skills and product knowledge make up only 15% of the ratio, they still cannot be overlooked. Lacking either of these is akin to having a car without any engine. No matter what, the car won't go anywhere. Same is true in sales. To succeed you must combine the 80% with the 15% and be improving both continually. Always be sharpening your skills and improving your product knowledge, and each day continue to apply the strategies presented in this book.

Immersion

The 15% talks specifically about skill and product knowledge. To continually enhance your skills and expand your knowledge, there is one technique that trumps the rest. This technique applies to every field of study and that is immersion. You can immerse yourself by reading books about selling, listening to instructional audio programs, subscribing to related trade journals, talking to friends about sales, role playing different sales scenarios, attending classes, reading reports, etc. The list really goes on and on. The key is to identify which of these appeals to you and then to schedule time to review them. For example, you can read books when at home, but when you are driving, listening to an audio program makes more sense. You can schedule training events on weekends, and watch educational videos at your desk during lunch.

Do you know that as much as 90% of salespeople have never read a book or taken a course on selling? As an extra mile salesperson don't ever let this be you. Continue to invest the time in yourself and your business by becoming truly knowledgeable about your offering. Reading this book is a great first step!

In my career selling cars, I immersed myself by reading all of the product manuals and watching corresponding product knowledge videos when they were available. I also researched the vehicles online, read consumer reports, and inspected each vehicle thoroughly. Next, I would role play before I

67

went on to sell on the selling floor. Frequently, I sold cars to my parents, girlfriend, and friends in role plays before I ever sold them for real. Remember, to make use of immersion and role play, the key is to schedule it.

Preview:

In the next chapter, we will build off of the preceding four concepts by determining in advance the goals we intend to achieve by apply this philosophy of selling.

Attitude is contagious, do I want to catch yours?

Chapter Summary:

1. 80% of your success in sales and in life is based on the inside i.e. your mindset, psychology, attitude, etc.
2. 15% of your success is based on your skills.
3. Only 5% of your success is influenced by the economy, the season, the perceived marketplace.
4. People want to do business with positive people.
5. Selling on the Extra Mile requires energy. Cultivate habits of exercise, nutrition, and positive thinking which will increase your energy.
6. Talk positive and you will become positive.
7. Choose positive vocabulary when speaking to yourself and others.
8. Focus on solutions, instead of problems.
9. Immerse yourself in your industry by reading trade journals, and joining trade associations and other organizations that support your field.
10. Role play sales scenarios regularly.

Chapter Five

Key Concept #5

Think Big, Sell Big!

An early mistake I made in my life and in my sales career was failing to set large enough goals. In fact, the biggest mistake most people make, who actually set goals, is setting them too small.

Goals have a magical quality of being able to move physical matter in two distinct directions. First, a well formulated goal moves you in the direction of the goal by affecting your thinking and your behavior. However, there is a second part that is often overlooked. Having a specific goal that you are moving towards has a tendency to begin to move people and things consistent with achieving that goal towards you. The reason why setting goals has the magnetic ability of bringing the right circumstances to you could be easily explained by pointing out how the goal inspires you to perform in a manner consistent with achieving the goal such as, attending the right meetings, saying the right things, and hanging out with the right people. Those people in turn take notice and consciously or not they begin to help you achieve your goal. Or setting goals simply evokes a magnetic power impossible to describe but part of our magnetic universe and usually associated with the universal Law of Attraction.

Whatever the reason, here are the facts. No goals have no power; and little goals possess little power to move you or the universe, so set Big Goals! Big goals have the inherent power to aid in manifesting big things!

In addition to setting big goals, which I am going to explain how to do in a moment, it is also important to have many goals for each area of your life and business. In my previous book, Warrior of Life, I devote an entire chapter to the practice of setting goals in all areas of your life. In this particular chapter, I am going to be focusing solely on setting goals specific to your business.

When I began selling cars, my initial goal was to sell as many cars as the top salesperson. It took me a long time, but eventually I became that top salesperson. If I knew then what I know now, I would have applied the following goal setting strategies in my life, and am certain this would have had a measurable impact on my selling efforts, and I would have become the best salesperson much sooner.

Set 3 Distinct Goals for Your Business

There are three distinct types of goals which you want to determine and establish for your business. **The first type of goal you want to set is your** *major goal.* The *major goal* must be a target far beyond your current level. If you can achieve the goal with your current skills and resources, then it is not anywhere near being big enough. In fact your major goal must propel you to jump levels. Now you may be wondering, what do I mean by levels?

In life and particularly in business, there are levels of success that people ascribe to other people for various reasons. The most common level of success is that of the owner of a company or CEO. This person is typically seen as being on a much higher level than the entry level (pay attention to those words entry level) salesperson.

71

Your major goal is your big goal and long term goal both rolled into one, and involves jumping levels. An ideal major goal for the entry level salesperson is to be CEO, or to own his own company. By setting this goal and really committing to it in the mind, this person will take on behaviors consistent with that goal, and leading the company in sales will just be one part of it.

If you are a CEO and you are reading this, you should want all of your employees to be CEO's. Not so they can take your job, but perhaps so they can launch new divisions, franchises, or other branches of the company. This is how you jump levels from CEO of one company, to Chairman of a major conglomerate.

If I had set the goal of owning my own dealership when I began selling cars, then it would have necessitated my developing other behaviors and learning different competencies that would have had a direct impact on my sales. For example:

- I would have looked at every prospect as a life-time customer and treated them as such in my conduct and follow-up.
- I would have learned everything I could about the service department, parts department, and other areas of the dealership.
- I would have asked for mentoring advice from the owner and manager's thus opening myself up to specialized knowledge.
- I would have operated as a 24/7 professional from day one.

Of course, I would have learned and applied all the teachings appearing in this book much sooner. Each of these strategies on their own would have had a significant impact on my daily sales, as they will for anyone who applies them.

So the first step is to set a major goal of leading the organization you work for, starting your own, or something similar. If you don't have the desire to succeed in a major way in the industry you're in, if you can't see yourself leading the company you are selling for, find something else to do, or somewhere else to work.

Setting a major goal works in conjunction with the next type of goal. **The second type of goal is your *yearly earnings goal*.** Deciding in advance how much money you intend to make, and thus how many sales you must make in order to achieve your goal is a crucial step in calibrating your mind and behavior in the direction of your goals.

Since this book is designed to help you triple your results, an effective yearly earnings goal to set for yourself should be at least 3x what you are earning now. Use this book, especially the first two chapters to enable you to generate 3x the prospects allowing you to close 3x the amount of sales you are closing now, thereby earning 3x more than you currently earn.

The third type of goal is your *daily goal*. The *daily goal* is a key concept that is seldom practiced. Unfortunately, too many people don't have any goals. Those who do will often write them down once and then put them in a drawer without referring to them on a regular daily basis. *Successful sales-people however, realize the power of establishing a daily goal consistent with their major goal, and in the direction of their yearly earnings goal.*

For example, if your yearly earnings goal is $250,000, and you divide that by fifty working weeks, you come up with your weekly goal. Now take that amount and divide it by the number of selling days in a week and then you will have your daily earnings goal. Now determine how many or how much you have to sell to achieve that daily earnings goal? Commit each and every day to selling that much and achieving the specific earnings goal you have established for yourself and your business.

To improve your focus on your goal, a great practice is to begin every day by writing your major goal, your yearly earnings goal, and your daily goal on the back of business card. Then, put the card where you will see it regularly throughout the day, such as in your wallet or cellular phone case. Each time you see it, take a moment to visualize yourself achieving your specific goals.

Daily Success Ritual

In my previous book, I wrote in detail the importance of cultivating a daily success ritual. The success ritual I described begins in the morning right after rising and includes meditation, visualization, and affirming goals. Recently, Fast Company ran an article called What Successful People Do with the First Hour of their Work Day (Kevin Purdy 8/22/2102, www.fastcompany.com) that takes my concept a step further. In this article, they recommend taking time to focus on the various things you are grateful for, to review your goals and tasks for the day, and then to begin at once without distraction to complete the most important task.

Every single day, usually before jumping out of bed in the morning, I take a moment to establish my daily goal in my mind. I then dwell on that goal while in the shower, eating breakfast, and driving to the office. Once there, I typically do as I just suggested and write down my daily goal on the back of my business card and keep it on my person to refer to it throughout the day. Do the same and watch your business flourish.

The Game of Selling

In interviewing successful sales leaders from a variety of different industries, one thing I discovered that they all shared is a fierce competitive streak. Each expressed a desire of wanting to be the best in their company, their territory, and even their entire industry. Many were former high school and collegiate athletes who discovered in sales the opportunity to compete on a different stage, employing the fundamental strategies of practice, rehearsal, and competitive play that they enjoyed in sports.

This philosophy of looking at your vocation of selling as a game is a terrific strategy. Infusing play into your work brings with it a quality of fun and enjoyment that attracts people to you. Plus, a healthy bi-product of competition is greater achievement and growth.

My recommendation is for you to think of every sales call as a competitive game. Realize, it is not a competition with the customer, that is the furthest thing from it. Your competition is with your peers in both your own company and in competing companies; they are the opponents. Helping the customer is the object of the game. To help the customer best solve their challenge results in the sale. Like any game, the best salespeople keep track of their stats e.g. number of customer calls, sales presentations, and orders, and endeavor to surpass them daily.

Chapter Summary:

1. Set goals that inspire you. Set goals which require you to put in the "extra" effort needed to achieve them.

2. The reason you set a goal is not for what you get, but for what it makes you to achieve it. As I said, when I was selling cars, I should have set the goal to be best salesperson in the country. Or own my own dealership. Later, when I finally applied this concept, my results where staggering. Set Big Goals!

3. Ask yourself how much do you want to earn? Then determine, what do you have to do to achieve it? Triple it!

4. Each day have a daily goal. That is potentially 27 daily goals per month (Even God rests one day a week).

5. Keep track of your stats such as number of customer calls, sales presentations, and orders, and endeavor to surpass them daily.

Section Summary:

These were the 5 main concepts my father shared with me which had a direct and positive effect on my results. Next, we are going to combine this philosophy with specific communication techniques to influence buyers to make a decision. Lastly, we will put this all together in a sales process which can be leveraged to lead the customer in the direction of making a selection and deciding to buy from you.

Section 2

Human Relations and Influence

Communication is the master skill in selling. Often, the average salesperson communicates in exactly the same manner with all prospects. However, psychologists have identified at least four distinct personality types, each with their own characteristics; one of which is the primary type for each individual. In addition, each person has their own unique way of processing information relating to which of their sensory faculties is the strongest. As a result, if you are communicating with each person in the same manner, all things being equal, you are only in sync with one out of four at best. To go the extra mile means to adjust and manipulate your communication style to better relate to the person you are endeavoring to do business with at that moment. By doing this you make them more comfortable and increase your chances for making the sale.

Chapter 6

Communication Strategies of Master Salespeople

In this chapter, you will be trained to make use of four of the most cutting-edge communication strategies for selling utilized by master salespeople. These strategies will allow you to influence almost anyone. The purpose of this approach is not to manipulate or take advantage of the customer, but instead to put him at ease and make it easier for him to identify his reasons for making the purchase. These reasons are based on the specific needs the prospective customer is trying to satisfy and can be related to a particular problem or to a specific desire. In any case, helping the customer identify his own motivating factors by communicating with him properly will help the sales process to flow naturally. The four communication strategies of master salespeople are:

- **Gaining Instant Rapport** – physical and vocal.
- Identifying tangible **commonalities and affinities** such as shared viewpoints, interests, people in common, etc.
- Presenting information that appeals to their primary **sensory modality**.
- **Empathic Rapport** – seek to fully understand. Show empathy.

81

I. Gaining Instant Rapport

Rapport is a natural "liking" two people share when they find that they are in sync or appear to be on the same wavelength. Rapport is something that can occur spontaneously between two people or can be manufactured. The benefit of creating rapport is that it allows for greater communication and sharing of opinions and ideas. In creating superior human relationships during a sales call, it is of the utmost importance that you create rapport as rapidly as possible. Also, since we know that people buy from people they like and trust, you are half-way to the sale the minute you establish this mutual feeling of liking. We also know that people like people who are like themselves, so the first part of establishing rapport is to match up with the other person through techniques such as "mirroring."

There are several factors which determine how well you can create rapport. To identify those factors we simply must examine the communication which normally takes place between two people. Studies have shown that during a conversation, the impression of the message that is actually being received by the intended party is based more on the body language and tone of voice of the speaker than by the words he uses. In fact, in all spoken communication words account for very little of the total message.

Experts agree that the average person only recalls 5-8% of the words being spoken; however, the feelings felt during the communication can be remembered for a lifetime. This means that creating positive feelings of liking must begin by focusing on the body language and tone of voice. This is why the phrase, "I see what you are saying" is so common. The cliché, "who you are speaks so loudly I can barely hear what you are saying," also supports this point.

In establishing rapport, upwards of 70% will be based on body language, 20-25% on tone of voice and rate of speech, and only 5-8% on the words you choose. Keep these percentages in mind, as well as the importance of establishing rapport early in the communication.

To establish instant rapport, once you are face to face with a prospective customer, you must begin immediately to mirror in a natural way their body language. For example, if they sit down and lean back in their chair while speaking to you, mirror this by leaning back in your own chair. If their arms are crossed, cross your arms. Try to match body language as closely as possible.

You will discover, that in order to do this effectively you must maintain constant eye contact (which is another secret of enhanced communication). People trust people who maintain eye contact, the other half of the like/trust equation. To strengthen your gaze, don't just try to mirror and match up with their body language, pay even deeper attention, and try to pace their breathing.

Caution, when they move, don't move with them like a game of Simon Says, but instead naturally adjust positions a few moments after.

In addition to mirroring body language, next you want to match up with the prospect's tone of voice and rate of speech. By the way, of the two, rate of speech is more important to match than tone. People who speak slowly drive people who naturally speak fast, nuts. The opposite is also true. People who speak slowly are turned off by people who speak too rapidly.

The key to making this technique work is to simply ask an initial question, and then to pay attention to the way the prospect answers. When they answer, match their tone of voice and rate of speech.

Rapport Building vs. Discovering Personality Types

Always remember, people buy from people they like and trust, and people like and trust those people who are like themselves.

There is a ratio in most sales environments which states that the average salesperson will sell 3 out of every 10 prospects they meet. I actually think the ratio is closer to 3 out of every 12. All things being equal, here is why I believe this ratio has emerged and spans so many different industries.

Psychologists have long determined that each individual's personality can be classified into one of four distinct personality types. You have probably read or been exposed to various personality tests which usually try to classify a person as being either a driver or dominant personality, an expressive or communicative person, an analytical person motivated by facts, figures and details, like an engineer, or a more submissive and easy going personality. People demonstrate their personality by how they move, express themselves, and how they speak. In sales, we know that people are able to more easily influence those people who are like themselves. So all things being equal, out of every twelve prospects, three will share your personality type, thereby giving you an average close of 3 out of 12.

Now remember, the best way to be like someone is to match up their non-verbal cues to gain rapport, since body language affects so much of the communication taking place. Since people express their personality traits in their body language, tone of voice, rate of speech, and other manners of expression including eye contact, and facial iterations, **by matching up and establishing rapport, you are able to communicate in a way consistent with their personality type**.

Now that you know this, you don't have to learn all of the different personality types and their corresponding traits. Nor will you need to memorize the various personality types, or spend time analyzing where the prospect falls on a personality matrix. Instead, you can easily apply the rapport building strategies in this chapter to make the prospect comfortable and to allow him to make a decision much easier. By choosing to build rapport with every prospect, you will match up with more people, being able to sell different personality types with ease. So instead of selling only the three people out of every ten who are like you, you can now sell many more by attempting to be like them.

My Biggest Sale

The importance of rapport building is to make your customer feel more comfortable. However, these techniques can be used to make anyone feel more comfortable allowing them to be more communicative and less guarded.

For example, my wife is from Medellin, Colombia. She grew up and lived in Medellin until she was 18, which is when she came to the United States. I first met her when she was 22, and upon seeing her I was immediately entranced and asked her on a date. She didn't say yes at first, but after a few weeks of *persistent* effort, she finally agreed.

On our very first date, things did not seem to be going well. I knew this by analyzing her body language. For instance, she was leaning back in her chair, arms folded across her chest, speaking very slow, and her eyes squinting as she studied me trying to decide whether or not she liked me. I, on the other hand, was leaning forward across the table, speaking rapidly, with my hands moving in unison to what I was saying, all while asking her questions and telling her a little bit about myself.

Determining that the communication wasn't going well, my mind finally identified the challenge. I actually said to myself, "you are not building rapport." I had just recognized the difference in our body language, rate of speech, and tone of voice, so I immediately began to mirror and match up with her. In just a few moments, I felt the communication begin to improve as if we were now in sync. To test it I lowered my voice a little and leaned forward while speaking to her. She leaned forward as well and the communication continued. She felt more comfortable with me and we began to dialogue, learning more and more about each other. The commonalities we discovered through this and subsequent conversations were real, and as of this writing we have been happily married for the past eight years.

When I recount this story, at first people think I was trying to manipulate her. This is actually not true. If anything, I was manipulating myself to make her feel more comfortable. Of course, if from our conversation she discovered I wasn't her type, she would have decided not to go out with me again. Remember, the purpose of rapport building is always to make the other person feel at ease.

Telephone Rapport

We just discussed how a large part of building rapport is based on body language. However, when communicating or selling over the telephone, body language is no longer a critical factor. Instead, the phone rapport is determined based on the matching up of tone of voice and rate of speech. Consequentially, it becomes imperative that you listen attentively to match up with their tone and rate as quickly as possible.

Many years ago, I worked in a call center scheduling appointments to sell life insurance. At that point in my career, I had not been actively applying the techniques on rapport building as illustrated in this chapter. Instead, I would call the prospect and read my prepared script very rapidly. Speaking rapidly was easy and natural for me, it was the slowing down that was sometimes difficult. Fortunately, in the majority of cases I was successful in scheduling insurance sales appointments. Soon word got around the office, and I was asked to share my approach with the other agents.

On one particular evening, while making calls, a woman answered the phone who sounded like she hadn't spoken to someone in years. She sounded older, had a sweet soft voice like a grandma, and spoke very slowly. I figured she would be an easy person to convince to schedule a meeting, so I raised my arm to get the other agents' attention, and beckoned them over to my desk to watch me in action. I went through my script at the same fast pace as usual and asked her which time of day would work best to meet, to which she replied that she wasn't interested. I thought, no problem, this is the typical first response, so I fired a prepared question at her where the only answer was yes, and followed that by asking her a second time to choose a time for a meeting. Again she said no. I continued to try in vain, until the phone call was disconnected. There I sat befuddled as to why she didn't agree to meet. I had done everything as usual, and she sounded like an ideal candidate. That is when I pieced together my knowledge of communication and rapport building and made the following discovery:

Everyone I had ever called, even if they naturally spoke slowly, when they heard the telemarketer (me) on the phone would speed up trying to get me off the call. By speeding up, we would automatically become in sync. We'd have instant rapport. Then it was only a matter of time before they felt the connection and decided to agree to one of my requests to meet. In this particular case, this woman never sped up. Her tone, and more importantly, her rate of speech both stayed the same. Thus, there was no rapport. I can only imagine that all she heard was what sounded like a stereotypical salesperson trying to fast talk his way into an appointment.

From this experience, I determined that if I had matched up with her tone and rate of speech, while still delivering my script, I would have had a much greater chance of securing the appointment. As a result, I make it a point to always match up rate of speech and tone of voice with everyone I speak to, especially when speaking on the phone.

Note: If you utilize the telephone in your business, be sure to apply this technique. A natural positive by-product is that you will find yourself listening more intently in order to match up. This level of listening has a powerful effect on the intended recipient and will be discussed later in this chapter.

Application:

If in a store where they come to you, ***build rapport at the greeting***.

In B2B sales, when at the potential customer's office, ***match up the moment you meet them***.

The best way to gain control of a meeting and to analyze body language, tone, and how the customer relates, is to ***ask a question***.

Then, as they answer the question, ***match up*** with them, and establish instant rapport!

II. Commonalities and Affinities

Building trust is very important in selling. The more your prospect trusts you, the more open they will be in the communication. This openness will allow you to fully help them to satisfy their needs, overcome their challenges, and meet their desires. However, the longer it takes to build trust, the longer it will take in order to make the sale.

A rapid method for gaining trust is to identify people and common interests which you and the prospective customer share. This is why in most sales meetings, the salesperson will try to initiate small talk at the onset of the meeting. It is a natural inclination the salesperson feels to identify something in common to create liking. Even better, is if you can identify people and things in common prior to the sales meeting. This is one of the reasons why referrals are so powerful. A referral comes with a common shared affinity for another person.

Just like with obtaining referrals, the key to establishing an affinity or identifying commonalities is to start broad and narrow it down. For example, you can make small talk by identifying where in the world the prospect is from (broad), and then asking their specific hometown (narrow). This is often a good place to start versus asking them if they like fishing.

Another strategy which often proves to be even more effective is to identify commonalities in advance of the meeting, during an initial phone call for instance. For example, when telephone prospecting to businesses I would always open the call by mentioning some of the companies which we were working with, that were similar and recognizable to the prospect. When calling consumers, I would mention other people in their town which we have helped through our service.

This approach is very effective because our brains work by linking things together, and when you present a potential commonality, the other person goes to work linking it to themselves, and as a result since you presented it, linking you to them.

When I worked in the call center scheduling life insurance appointments, my list included where people lived. To establish a commonality, I would open my call by telling them that we worked in their town (only if it was true). For example, "my name is Chuck Householder from ABC Insurance Company, and I'm working with homeowners in your-town, USA." Just this single perceived commonality kept most people from initially hanging up, and allowed me to go further with my prepared script.

Later on, whenever I called on companies I would take the same approach I used when selling life insurance, but instead of the town, I would mention two to three of their competitors who I was already working with. In addition to the commonalities and perceived affinities this engendered, it would also garner their interest. I suppose this was because they too wanted to know what their competitors were doing.

A great strategy for building an affinity or being in a position to discover commonalties with a prospect is derived from the suggestion in chapter two, which was to join a trade organization. I already shared how I had joined the Direct Selling Association for the purpose of prospecting and networking; when I called DSA member companies I would always mention my membership since they were often members as well.

Key: To apply this approach, always be on the lookout for things you and your potential customers might share in common. In addition, try to discover in advance or during the meeting what other people you both may also know as well. Commonalities and an affinity for the same people are powerful tools for engineering mutual liking and trust.

III. Sensory Modalities

Sensory modalities describe the way that information is best received and encoded and presented to the brain. Of the five senses we all share, each individual person typically experiences everything that is happening in their life with a preferred sense. Some people for example, are more visual, meaning that they lead with their eyesight, and rely on visual clues to process information and to make decisions. Others are more auditory, and remember more of what they hear versus what they have seen; and, for these people words are very powerful. The third most common sense is the kinesthetic sense which relates to touch. This person relies on actual feeling of the thing in question, or their own emotional feelings to make a decision.

It is possible to determine a person's preferred sensory modality by paying attention to the words they use. You can simplify the process by asking specific types of questions that will help to narrow down their preferred sense for analyzing things in their world.

When you ask the following types of questions pay attention to how they respond. Then, once you know which sense they lead with, you can phrase all your questions in concert with their primary sensory modality.

*What are you **looking** for? How do you like this **look?***
*How do this **sound?** Would you like to **hear** our proposal?*
*Would you **feel** like trying this? How does this choice **feel**?*

The intention of identifying and directing communication in concert with their preferred modality is to make the customer more comfortable so they can make clear decisions.

It's important to realize that building rapport, identifying modality, determining commonalities, and asking thoughtful questions are all skills required to enable the customer to make a comfortable buying decision.

IV. Empathic Rapport: Ask Questions and LISTEN

Creating empathic rapport can also be described as *seeking to fully understand.* In order to create empathic rapport, it is best to have a prepared a thorough mental and written list of open-ended questions that allow the prospective customer to completely express their wants and needs.

Soon, as you develop more experience in questioning, you will know what to ask and what you will likely be asked. Keep this in mind, as too many salespeople don't live up to their potential because they talk too much. When selling, an effective approach is to behave like a great attorney. Great attorneys win cases by what they ask, not by what they say. A great attorney backs people into a corner with well planned questions.

As salespeople, we open our customers up to possibilities and opportunities with the questions we ask. The purpose of asking good questions is to expand the customer's level of awareness.

Key: To build empathic rapport, spend the bulk of your time with the customer asking targeted questions. Be totally engaged, interested and sincere by paying attention to how they answer.

3 Types of Questions to Prevent Indecision

As you determine which questions you are going to ask, be sure to build them around the following three topics. By asking questions relating to Time, People, and Money, you prevent indecision and stalling early in the engagement.

Time:
When are you planning to make a decision?
When must you take delivery?
When do you need it by?
By what date must you implement the solution?
When do you want to launch?
And of course, when do you want it? How about now?

91

People:

Who else is helping you choose the color?
Who will be helping you decide?
Is there anyone else you'd like to show this to?
Who will be on the team?
Who else will be using this product?
Who has to approve this purchase?

Money:

How much are you looking to invest?
What are your budget parameters?
How much have you allocated?
Where is the money coming from?

Whether selling electronics, cars, real estate, or a complex sale like a comprehensive marketing program, your initial questions must be about time, people, and money.

The best salespeople ask these types of questions up front. Mediocre or novice salespeople ask these questions after a product or service has been chosen, and by this time it is often too late.

Key: You always want to ask *time* questions early on. Make them part of the agenda starting with, "How much time do you have for this meeting today?"

Regardless of what you are selling, you want to discover very early on who the real decision makers are, or if it is a team effort. Asking the *people* specific questions will be very helpful in determining the decision making process. Also, if you don't have decision makers in front of you, go get them.

If your product or service has a specific price, determining in advance what the prospect is looking to invest allows you to present the choices most consistent with their budget. It also helps you to determine if you need to expand the amount of money they intend to invest.

Along with asking questions, comes effective listening. The number one quality on the list among the best of the best salespeople is that they go the extra mile in their listening. They give the customer their full attention. They listen with their eyes and their ears. Their body language indicates that they are engaged. They show agreement by nodding their head, and can paraphrase back what has been said. They totally seek to understand.

By the way, as I wrote in the introduction, applying these strategies and techniques in your everyday life will improve it as well. For example, if you listen better with your spouse and children, your family life will likely be better. They will appreciate you more, and will in turn feel valued and appreciated. So tonight, when you get home from work, don't tell them about your day, ask about theirs.

Exercise:

Put this practice to work in your everyday life. Be like a young child, and for a few days, ask questions incessantly to the point of annoyance. Find out everything. Why certain people do what they do? Why do they put cream in their coffee? Why they sit a certain way? What they think about on the way to work? Get comfortable being curious.

Next, LISTEN and ask even more follow-up questions.

By gauging their tone of voice and body language, you will be able to recognize non-verbal cues from them that indicate if you are pushing it. Pay attention, and have enough sense to know when to stop.

Finally, by putting this into practice, you will be developing sleuth like questioning skills which can be transferred and applied in your selling business.

Chapter Summary:

1. Practice the golden rule, and treat customers as you would want to be treated.
2. Successful people have empathy. They can relate. They can put themselves in the other person's shoes.
3. The benefit of creating rapport is it allows for greater communication and sharing of opinions and ideas.
4. In establishing rapport, upwards of 70% will be based on body language, 20-25% on tone of voice and rate of speech, and only 5-8% on the words you choose.
5. Building trust is very important in selling. The more your prospect trusts you, the more open they will be in the communication.
6. Of the five senses we all share, each individual person naturally experiences everything that is happening in their life with a preferred sense.
7. As salespeople we open people up to possibilities and opportunities with questions.
8. By asking questions relating to Time, People, and Money, you prevent indecision and stalling early in the engagement.

Section 3

How to SELL on the Extra mile Process

If you are in sales, selling a specific product or service, you must have a scripted sales presentation. Everything I have ever sold, ranging from gym memberships, to cars, to mortgages, required a scripted presentation. Often, the presentation that worked the best was broken down into phases that contained rehearsed specific questions, trial closes, and pre-determined steps toward enabling the customer to make a buying decision.

Even if you do a large portion of your sales presentations over the phone, it is wise to have a rehearsed scripted sales presentation for that as well. Following a script with the appropriate steps in place, better positions you to control the entire process.

The whole format of the forthcoming Selling on the Extra Mile process is geared towards helping the salesperson to take the customer to the point where they are continuously thinking about buying, and your script must do this.

In the next two chapters, we will look at combining rapport building with additional influencing techniques such as presenting your offering, and aligning it with their interests, needs, and wants, as you take your prospect through a pre-determined sales process. This process will serve as the framework for developing your own sales presentation with corresponding scripts. It is entirely acceptable if your presentation is nothing more than a personalization of the forthcoming sales process you will learn. In time you will personalize it even further as it grows organically.

Finally, once you have your complete sales presentation, or at least all the workable pieces are in place, role play it among your colleagues in order to refine each portion to make it better and more effective.

Your sales presentation should be alive and continually evolving ever so slightly into a new and better process. For example, if you find different customers are asking similar questions, or common objections are arising, reframe those questions and objections into statements to include in all of your presentations. This is just one example, of the many nuggets of wisdom you will discover in this section as you build your own Extra Mile presentation.

Chapter 7

Consumer Sales Process

Every master salesperson has a scripted or semi-scripted presentation tailored to selling their specific product or service. The following presentation strategy is meant to be the framework which can be customized based on your own offering and preferred approach. However, the following five steps are designed to be followed consecutively and serve to guide you along the path to closing the sale. Each step is crucial in developing trust, as well as determining and satisfying both the logical and emotional reasons why the potential prospect is interested in your offering.

Consumer Sales Process
1. **Greeting**
2. **Needs Analysis**
3. **Demonstrate**
4. **Build Support**
5. **Implement and Deliver**

1. Greeting (when you first meet them)

The first part of any sales approach begins with the *greeting*. The greeting sets the stage for the entire sales presentation. When selling a consumer product you typically don't have a specific written agenda for each prospect, especially when the prospect is a walk-in, or doesn't have an appointment (as is the case when selling in a store). As such, you need to set the stage for the prospect very early, and by *set the stage* I mean take control of the sale immediately. By gaining control, you are able to guide the prospect in a way that allows them to fully communicate their needs ensuring the proper selection of the product or service being offered.

The following are two main strategies that encompass the first stage of the consumer sales process:

One: Always Open with a Question

Once the formal introductions have taken place, the very next step is to ask a question. The person who asks questions is always in control. By opening with a question, you immediately gain control of the sales presentation. The key to making this strategy work is to have prepared opening questions specific to your offering. Here are a few types of questions/topics to incorporate into your sales process:

- Find out why are they here?
- What brought them here?
- What are they looking for?
- What is the purpose of the visit?
- What are they looking to accomplish?
- When are they looking to accomplish it?

Be able to demonstrate why you are there in your role as well. The previous sentence is meant to sound funny, sort of tongue-in-cheek. However, the intent behind that statement is serious. Make sure you conduct yourself as a professional. This means you must be completely versed in your solution. This can be accomplished through immersion; know everything you can about your product, industry, available incentives, etc.

Two: Match Up

Once you ask your initial question, immediately match up to gain rapport. This is key! Ask your opening question, and then pay attention to how they answer the question. What is their tone of voice like, what is their rate of speech? Match up with their body language. Apply the strategies for influence imparted in the previous chapter.

As you move through the following steps of the consumer sales process, continue to match up and mirror your customer, and, look to discover and express commonalities you both share. Additionally, pay attention to what sensory modality they lead with, and accommodate that in your communication.

2. Needs Analysis (Narrow it down)

A needs analysis is a part of every selling methodology. The purpose of the needs analysis when selling consumers is to *narrow down* their selection, and to keep narrowing it down until the exact option is selected. You accomplish this by continuing to ask detailed questions in order to fully understand the specific need or desire which is creating the motivation in the prospect to trade their money for your offering. The needs analysis is where you gain empathic rapport through questioning. Also, don't make the mistake of moving to the price negotiation until a specific product or service is chosen by the prospect as the one he wants to buy.

On the next page are the two main strategies that encompass the second stage of the consumer sales process:

One: Go to the nearest model

Go to the nearest model when selling a product. If selling a service, grab a brochure unless something more tangible is available. When selling a TV for example, go to the nearest model, touch it and begin asking specific questions pertaining to the customer's interests, desires, and needs.
Some sample questions to ask initially are:

- What model are you looking for?
- What features do you desire?
- How will you be using it?

Two: Time, People, Money

As presented in the previous chapter, ask questions about the three most influential buying factors which are Time, People, and Money. These types of questions are critical for setting the proper selling stage.

Be sure to ask questions as soon as appropriate that relate to Time, People, and Money. For example:

- When are you looking to purchase? (Time)
- Who else is helping you choose? (People)
- What are your budget parameters? (Money)
- How much can you afford to invest? (Money)

3. Demonstrate Product

Asking questions are a constant throughout any good sales process. Once you've determined a direction based on the information you gained in phase two of the process, continue to narrow down the selection by demonstrating the product.

The purpose here is to solidify the specific model and features the customer wants while building value for your offering. If your offering is a service, it is to clearly determine the various components of the service the customer desires.

Remember, the goal of this part of the process is to build value and *confirm* which specific product or service offering the customer intends to buy. Specificity is key. Without a specific choice, no emotional bearing can be established between the customer and the offering.

Next, you will learn a method of relating features and benefits of your offering to the prospective customer that is used by the master sales professionals. Instead of the typical features/benefits presentation, the master salesperson adds three additional components that help get to the core of the customer's desire for your offering.

FABE, plus Question?

Now is the time to talk about how to demonstrate a product/service in the most effective manner possible. The preferred method to apply is called: *FABE, plus question?*

F stands for Feature – This is the starting off point. Select a primary feature(s) to discuss, especially those that the customer mentioned an interest in, and also those which offer you a competitive advantage.

A stands for Advantage – Next, point out the advantage to them of having this feature. For example, the benefit of a TV remote control is that it doesn't require you to move from your seat when selecting a new channel. This builds up to the next point...

B stands for Benefit – Every customer wants to know the benefits; mainly how this feature will improve their lives in some way, and most importantly what are the specific benefits of this choice over others? Be sure that you are speaking specifically to them, meaning that you discuss their benefits, not yours.

E stands for examples – Use stories, and paint pictures in the customer's mind when describing benefits. Don't tell them, show them with a story. Stories have selling power. Having a handful of positive, influential stories in your quiver which helps the customer to experience in their imagination the advantages and benefits of your offering is very powerful at motivating them to act.

Note: Grab credibility materials. When discussing FABE have a brochure or catalog handy. People believe what is in writing. Of course, it goes without saying that you ensure everything in writing is 100% accurate.

Plus Question – This step is crucial, and is often left out by the majority of salespeople, who more often than not will rattle off a laundry list of features without ever confirming value with the prospect.

Plus Question means to follow up each *example* by asking a question to confirm understanding and to continue to narrow down their selection. Sample questions might be:

- Can you see any additional ways this feature can be useful to you?
- How good does this feature sound?
- What impact do you feel this could have?
- Of these benefits, which is most important to you?

4. Build Support (Personalizing)

Building support means getting them to fully agree that the product or service you are presenting to them is the specific choice they want to buy. At this step in the process, the way in which you narrow down their selection is by *personalizing* it to them whenever you speak. This allows you to deliver supporting statements and examples that reinforce their choice.

For example, in the needs analysis you may have asked, "how will you be using this in your home?" They in turn would have provided the answer. Now, you are able to reinforce their answer by personalizing their selection, thus building support for them to buy. The answer will go something like this, "When this is in your home, here is how this will improve, solve, fix, enhance..."

Stories Sell

This part of the process presents another opportunity to build value for your product or service by telling rehearsed stories of a previous customer's success. Stories help to paint a picture in the mind of the prospective customer of how to best use a particular solution. Using examples of previous clients who have experienced success is the easiest way.

I can't stress enough the value of having several anecdotes to choose from in which to relay to the prospective customer to drive a benefit home in their mind. Gathering written testimonials from past clients which tell a story is even more powerful in creating a persuasive picture in the customer's mind.

In the sales process, listening is a most important quality, but telling perfectly timed stories closes deals. This is Key!

Also, this is the point in the process to discuss other components which will personalize the selection to them, but couldn't have been presented until a selection was chosen. This might include other value-added benefits that come complimentary with a product or service. For example, in selling cars, this would be the point that I would show other areas of the dealership in which the prospect would find benefit once they became a customers such as free loaner cars, discounts on parts, complimentary oil changes, and similar offerings.

Next, is the final stage in the consumer sales process.

5. Implement and Deliver

I don't call this stage the close or closing, I purposefully call it *Implement*. Selling on the Extra Mile is all about building a long term relationship. This begins with the greeting and extends way past the signed contract to the implementation or pick-up/delivery of the product/service, and continues on to future sales and ongoing referrals.

We should always expect that since they are at our location (at the store, bank, business, etc.) they are buying even if they initially say otherwise. When I began my career selling cars, I expected that everyone who came to the dealership was there to buy, so I would ask questions throughout the process that demonstrated my assumption. I couldn't imagine that someone would have nothing better to do for an hour or more, that they would sit through an entire presentation for a product they had no intention of buying. The fact is they wouldn't. They may not intend to purchase your offering that very moment, but that is why there is this process and the questions about Time, People, and Money. All of this is designed to help them make an informed buying decision, and to discover how they could implement your product or service immediately, instead of at some later date.
Note: It is important throughout this stage, be thinking in your mind both implementation and delivery. (Consumer products are typically delivered.)

Implementation Questions

In the previous four steps, and especially at this point in the process, it is imperative to be asking what are called *implementation questions*, also referred to in sales as "trial closes."

For example, at the car dealership, I would work into the conversation implementation questions such as:

- How are you going to be registering your new car?
- When do you plan to take delivery?
- What additional features do you want added prior to delivery?

These types of questions are valuable and make up a very vital part of persuading or influencing someone. The reason is because, **in order to answer a properly formed implementation question, the prospect must accept in their mind (at least for the moment) that they are indeed going to buy the offering.** The more convinced the customer becomes that they are going to buy, through answering a series of implementation questions, the easier the sale becomes.

When forming implementation questions, it is important to personalize them for the customer. For example, in terms of selling automobiles, asking the prospect if they are going to be putting running boards on their new truck, is a great example of personalizing the product for them. Also, whenever you personalize something and the customer accepts it, they are making a choice in their mind that reinforces their decision to buy. The fact is that in order to answer the previous question they have to accept in their mind that they are buying the truck. If they have trouble answering the question, or are unsure, it may be a sign that you've chosen the wrong selection. You can determine this by asking more implementation questions.

The more implementation questions you are able to ask (in which the customer can only answer, if in their own mind they see themselves purchasing your offering) the more certain your customer will become in choosing to purchase your offering.

Deliver

Once the customer has selected the *exact* product or service for their particular needs, and are desiring to take delivery at a specified time, simply write up the order and hand it to them while asking them to sign it (thus completing the process).

In the next chapter, the fifth step which is also *Implementation* will include in the description a strategy for selling when the price is being negotiated or is by nature negotiable.

*In Chapter 8, a slightly different process will be introduced which is designed to be the basis for sales professionals calling on buyers for a business. This could be the CEO, or a top officer for small, medium, and large size companies. These buyers usually have different buying motives than the individual consumer who is making a purchase for personal use.

However, regardless of what you sell, it is important that you familiarize yourself with both processes. This is for a variety of reasons. For example, representatives from a company go to consumer retail stores often to make large purchases for the business. An example might be a business owner buying twenty cell phones for the employees to use to conduct business. Another example is the purchasing representative from a company visiting the local car dealership to buy a dozen fleet vehicles. These are just two reasons why, understanding the mind of the business buyer and the similarities and differences which make up both selling processes is important.

Bonus Strategy: Linking

When you are presenting to a prospective customer, at the forefront of your mind you want to be continually seeking to discover the underlying WHY behind every choice they are making. Why do they want this product vs. a similar version? Why are they in the market now? Why did they decide to visit your store? Why do they want a certain feature?

Discovering the *why* behind a person's desire for something is valuable. It is the *why* that needs to be satisfied with the *what,* which is the product or service you sell. Once you discover their *why*, their underlying motivation, then you can tailor your demonstration and build support specifically towards their individual needs and wants.

The way you do this is simply to continually *link* the answers to your *why* questions, with the respective Feature, Advantage, Benefit, and Example you provide when demonstrating your offering.

For instance, when a customer told me that one of their *why's* when choosing to look at our fuel efficient cars was to save money on gas, I would *link* saving money as a particular benefit to all of the features that enabled the low gas mileage. For instance, I might say, "these particular tires provide a smooth driving experience, which provides comfort on long trips and helps improve fuel efficiency. This specific engine design provides great acceleration without wasting fuel. The following long-life maintenance features will save *x* dollars over the course of three years."

Linking is an example of applying empathic rapport to the sales process. By listening attentively and seeking to fully understand, and then by demonstrating that understanding through verbally linking the customer's specific motivation to your solution, you create a powerful level of rapport.

Chapter Summary:

1. The first part of any sales approach begins with the greeting.
2. The person who asks questions is always in control.
3. As you move through this process, apply the communication strategies imparted in chapter six.
4. For each feature of your product/service, know the advantage this feature presents, the benefit this feature provides, and an example of how this benefit can be derived.
5. After presenting each feature ask a question to gain agreement (trial close).
6. Think implement vs. close.
7. Discover the *why* behind your customer's want.

Chapter 8

B2B Sales Process

Business customers are used to meeting with salespeople and as such have come to expect an adequate level of professionalism. Superstar sales professionals, those who go the extra mile, make it their intention to exceed those customers' expectations. They do this by committing to a standard of excellence far beyond what the customer is used to. They demonstrate their commitment in the quality of their research, the time they arrive, the level of their questions, and the steps they take to solving their customer's challenges. The following B2B sales process has been designed to enable you to exceed your customer's expectations, thereby positioning yourself more favorably against the competition, allowing you to more easily win the sale.

Whereas in the consumer sales process, the objective is to choose a specific selection and then to reinforce the customers emotional and logical motivations for buying it, in the B2B sale, the objective is to identify the specific challenge or need present and then to position your offering as the solution to that need. You will discover how to do this in this chapter, as well as come to understand that there are really three underlying needs that are inherent in a business sale, and once you discover which particular need is present, you will be positioned to better satisfy that need and make the sale.

B2B Sales Process:

    1.   **Intelligence Gathering and Pre-Call Planning**
    1.5   *Thirty Minute Rule*
    2.   **Greeting and Agenda**
    3.   **Needs Analysis**
    4.   **Solve**
    5.   **Implement**

1. Intelligence Gathering

This isn't part of most documented sales processes and therefore its importance usually isn't stressed. In Selling on the Extra mile we realize that the sales presentation actually begins at the research stage. The information you are able to discover by performing thorough research prior to the meeting will prove to be extremely valuable when you are meeting with the decision makers face to face.

It is imperative that you do your research and pre-call planning prior to every meeting. Never go to a meeting until you've done thorough intelligence gathering. Be like a secret agent and endeavor to discover as much as you can about your target company. Begin by using Google to search for online information about their company. Next, search their primary website, read their news releases, see what job openings they have (this can tell you a lot about the company), and research the key people, especially the person you are meeting with.

For example, when I was selling marketing and PR programs, I was targeting a major company in North Carolina. To gain access to the C-level suite decision makers, I would often network and ask for referrals, as suggested in this book. However, in this case, my networking wasn't delivering so I was relying on cold calls starting with the CEO and working my way down the organizational chart.

Before every telephone prospecting call, I would take a moment to visit their website. One particular day, I saw an intranet article that talked about their company mandate to drive sales. I immediately recognized how our programs could have a direct impact on helping them to achieve their specific goals. I developed a quick script and immediately called the Executive Vice-President of Sales, who was leading the charge. I got his assistant on the phone and explained to her how I can help the EVP complete his assignment. She took the message, and forty-five minutes later the EVP called me and we scheduled an in-person meeting. This example demonstrates how research is extremely valuable in both prospecting as well as before the actual sales meeting. It's worth repeating: research, research, research. Also, always be immersed in your industry.

By the way, I eventually got the sale!

1.5 Thirty Minute Rule

Always plan to arrive at the sales meeting thirty minutes early. Once you arrive at their office, invoke the power of the Law of Attraction by taking the time to visualize the sales meeting going great. Do this while waiting for the meeting time to arrive. Also, try to get a feel for the layout of the office park. Watch the people coming and going from the building. Additionally, use this time to relax and completely prepare for the upcoming meeting.

Next, once you enter the office, be sure to make friends with receptionist. Use this opportunity to ask additional questions in order to gain further information.

Finally, and most importantly, when the meeting does finally begin you are relaxed, poised and ready.

Warning: Never be late for a sales meeting. This will ruin their impression of you and will have a devastating effect on your potential to make a sale. The thirty minute rule helps to prevent that from happening.

2. Greeting and Agenda

Greeting: When you meet the person for the first time your strategy is to apply the influencing techniques covered in chapter six, and that is to create rapport immediately. Pay attention to and mirror their body language. Match their tone of voice and rate of speech. Seek to gain instant rapport at the moment you meet. Then, as the meeting progresses, pay attention to which sensory modality they lead with, and look to identify things you share in common.

Agenda: Be sure to always bring your tools to the meeting. In sales, our tools are usually our attaché with notepad, pens, brochure, and list of questions, plus a *prepared agenda for the meeting.*

Be sure to have a prepared agenda for every meeting. This simple document puts you in control of the sales meeting, and allows it to unfold according to your terms. In my career providing sales management and coaching, you would not believe how many people I have met who did not prepare a written agenda for their meetings. The agenda is crucial for setting the tone and gaining control of the meeting. The agenda need not be complex either. Make it simple. Here are the three key components of any agenda:

1. Find out what they want. Why did they decide to meet?
2. Tell them what you want. How your company wants to help.
3. Indicate your process to *meeting* what both parties want.

Even if you plan to verbalize the agenda, it is always helpful to have it written down as well. People seldom argue with the written word.

Quick tip: Have all of your rates and pricing in writing as well. If price is an issue for the prospective customer, let them know that you will customize the product or service to meet their needs, and thus the price will be customized as well. However, by putting your rates in writing, this naturally has shown to be a deciding factor in limiting the discount during the negotiation.

3. Needs Analysis

{**From Chapter 7:** A needs analysis is a part of every selling methodology. The purpose of the needs analysis is to continue to ask detailed questions in order to fully understand the specific need or desire which is creating the motivation in the prospect to trade their money for your offering.}

In B2B sales, there are several other factors which can be motivating the purchase of a product or service to benefit the business. Since, in this case the offering won't be for personal use as in consumer sales, the purpose of the needs analysis is to identify the challenges that can be solved, and also to identify and cater to those motivating factors.

I have discovered three factors which necessitate a buying decision in B2B sales. These three factors are usually the driving force *underlying* the buyer's willingness to invest in a product or service. I call these underlying factors **The 3 P's.**

The first P is Perception. The decision maker in a business may choose one company's product or service over another based on how the selection will be perceived by his peers, and, how it will affect how he is perceived. Choosing a certain product that improves production, decreases costs, and improves revenues would seem like a natural choice, however, for some buyers if the product doesn't improve their standing in the company in some perceivable way, they won't even bother. Identifying if a prospective buyer is motivated by perception is key in helping you to respond to their needs.

The second P is for Productivity. If the decision maker's concern is primarily about improving efficiencies, and driving up production, or shortening the manufacturing process, then most likely you are dealing with someone whose underlying need is productivity. Often, those prospects whose job function is close to the production forces in their company, whether those production forces are assemblers, or outside sales reps, will base their decision on the product or service's ability to improve and increase productivity.

However, realize that some buyers choose to purchase solutions that improve productivity because those improvements will enhance their perceived standing in the company (as mentioned in the paragraph on Perception). Asking thorough questions about what is driving their decision, allows you to present your offering in a way that caters to their specific underlying factor (linking).

The third P is Price. Price buyers are interested in cash in, and cash out. An increase in perception and production are nice, however, if the product or service doesn't have a direct influence on improving the bottom line, they won't invest.

Often in an organization the people who want the product aren't the people who can buy it. That may be left up to the purchasing department, or someone who is prized in the organization for their negotiating skills. If you know that price is front and center in the mind of this buyer, then you can talk cash in, cash out, ROI, and discounts versus productivity and perception, in order to be more persuasive.

Ask and Listen

To discover the underlying motivating buying factors, as well as all of the buying criteria it is vital to perform a thorough needs analysis. To perform a thorough needs analysis, imagine you are speaking to a close friend and have a sincere desire to help them. Begin by asking open ended questions and then narrow down their challenges by asking closed ended questions. Open ended questions allow them to elaborate. Close ended questions allow you to gain specificity in understanding their challenges.

Just as presented in the consumer sales process, ask questions initially that pertain to Time, People, and Money.

Then ask questions which help you determine their underlying driving force – the Three P's – such as Perception, Production, and Price. To do this, simply phrase your question in a way that helps you gauge what is most important to them.

For example:

- "What is most important to you when choosing…"
- "Which would you prefer…"
- "What benefits do you hope to get from…"

Shortcut: Whenever the prospective customer presents a problem or challenge to you which embodies the need, ask them **why** they believe the problem is happening.

"Why do you think this is happening?"
This is one of the best needs analysis questions you can ask.

Finally, ask several WHY questions in order to narrow down the specific underlying factors driving their motivation to possibly invest in your company's offering.

4. Solve

This stage is the most important part of the process. Even if you do a spectacular needs analysis, if you can't articulate how your offering is going to meet the customer's needs and solve their problems, you will lose to someone who can better describe it.

However, there is a way to stack the odds in your favor and that is by presenting your solution to the customer in a manner that makes it appear in their thinking that they have already purchased. Essentially, the aim is to personalize your solution to the customer and describe it as if they are using it, or have been using it already.

For example, when I sold PR programs, we had a specific process that would take place once we received the signed agreement. So prior to the sale, whenever I presented our solution to the customer, I spoke as if we had already received their signed agreement and were implementing the solution for them. For instance, we would always have a kick-off meeting for every new client, so using this approach I would ask them well in advance of their having agreed to become a client, "who (from your company) would you like on the kickoff call?" When I sold cars, I would ask well before they signed the dotted line, "would you like running boards installed on your new SUV?"

Now here is the magic: in both examples, in order to answer the question, the customer has to accept in their mind (at least for a moment) that they have purchased the product or service being offered. This will accomplish one of two desirable outcomes. Either they will go ahead and accept the offering and move through the process to the point of confirming that acceptance by signing a purchase agreement, or they will object to the question helping to illicit their preferences. In either case you are able to move the sale to the point of implementation.

Here are two additional tactics to use when presenting your solution to solve their challenges in this stage:

Keep it Simple

Don't make the solution sound too complicated. Make sure you are able to describe your company, your products and services, as well as trends in your industry in a way that a child would understand. This means, be sure to define complex terms, regardless of who you are speaking to.

Keeping it simple is a surefire way to gain friendly business relationships. Remember, a confused mind always says no!

A confused mind always says no!

Stories Sell in B2B Sales

This is worth repeating - Stories sell. Have several rehearsed stories to tell, as well as client testimonials to share in order to paint a picture in the prospective client's mind about the benefits and advantages of your solution. Always follow-up a story, and/or example, with a question that confirms the prospective customer's agreement.

One of the best sales professionals I know, who has been selling to survive since he was just 8 years old, when he invested in his first job, a treacherous paper route, is a master at using stories to sell. He uses stories to demonstrate his products and services, and also uses stories to handle objections. He paints a vivid picture with words in the mind of his prospective customer, while also using those words to reach their heart. By stirring their emotions, he inspires them to take actions that they may have delayed taking.

Now here is the key; often the story he tells is a depiction of what might be possible in the future if the prospective customer does business now. In other words, he paints an attractive future in the mind of the prospect.

Paint an attractive future in the mind of the prospect that they can derive from the purchase of your product or service.

A top financial planner I worked with, when we were selling college investment plans, would paint the picture to parents (prospective customers) of their sitting at a university graduation ceremony sometime in the future, watching their child walking across the stage to accept their degree. He'd then ask them, how they think they will be feeling at that time? Next, he would *link* that positive future image and the associated feeling back to the minimal investment required now to create the possible future scene.

Take a moment now and consider how you can do the same thing when presenting your product or service. What are the future benefits that can be enjoyed by companies that purchase your offering? What are the enhancements in perception that can be had by the decision maker who chooses to do business with you? The answers to these questions and the images they evoke presented in a story format are how you solve a customer's challenge.

Once the solution has been determined, the final step is next.

5. Implement

Selling on the Extra Mile goes well beyond the close to the implementation stage. However, it is at this point that the final details of the agreement are called into question, and it is where some sales professionals tend to get held up.

In automotive sales we had a very simple way to expedite this part of the process. Once we had selected a vehicle, chosen all of the features, were reviewing the selection and about to discuss price, the salesperson would say immediately after vocally confirming the selling price, "in purchasing this car NOW, how would you like the title to read?" Notice, how this question assumes the close, and goes right into implementation.

Next, even if the customer objected to the price, the follow-up question was, "we will get the price right; when would you like to take delivery of the car, how about NOW?"

Once the title information and the delivery time and date were agreed upon, the next step was simply to negotiate the best price.

In most sales methodologies, this is the part of the process in which the salesperson whips out a glossary of closes. Unfortunately, many of these closes are so tried, that the customer has heard them all before, and they get turned off. An example of this type of worn out close is the Ben Franklin

Close. In the Ben Franklin Close, the salesperson describes a method Franklin is presumed to have used to make decisions, and that is by listing the pro's and con's down opposite sides of the same piece of paper. If the pro's outweigh the con's, the customer then should buy. How ridiculous. The salesperson must be cringing every time a con is listed; and the customer must be laughing when there are thirty pro's and only three con's.

In Selling of the Extra Mile, the whole process is geared towards implementation, so the approach is to give the prospective customer *implementation choices*. In other sales systems this would be called *closing*.

Implementation Choices

Continuing with the example of buying a car, the salesperson would now present two different purchasing options, and allow the customer to choose one. If the customer still objects to the price, the salesperson asks what figure the customer desires, and then presents additional choices. If the customer doesn't object to those options, or even the initial choices, then they will have chosen a purchasing option and the deal is finalized.

This approach of giving at least two choices, usually works the best regardless of what you are selling. By giving implementation choices, you are able to determine several factors regarding the price. The first is if price is not an issue. This will be demonstrated when they make a choice. The second is if their budget is the issue. Though this should have been brought out earlier when questions about Time, People, and Money were first asked (of course the prospect may have been holding back). The third is if it isn't price at all, if something else is missing, this will come up at the moment you ask them to choose an option. Lastly, if price is the issue and they intend to negotiate further, giving them a choice in no way says that those are the only choices, and allows the prospective customer to counter offer.

If the product or service you offer has a fixed cost, you can still take advantage of this option by giving a choice of payment terms. This is a great approach because it takes the prospective customer's focus from the

119

price to the methods of paying for the offering. For instance, when I sold recruiting services to companies, I would quote them a price and then as part of the quote, I would also give them two payment methods to choose from. Next, I would take their focus from the price by asking, "which of the two methods would work best for you?" When they picked one, I would simply write it down on the agreement, and then hand the agreement to them asking them to sign it.

In this stage, the choice is between two prices, or perhaps two financing options; what it is not between is a certain price and nothing at all. By offering choices, you and your customer are teamed up as allies. You are now seen as a consultant or trusted advisor versus a typical salesperson. Essentially, by giving your customer options you move yourself from across the table, to sitting alongside them. Then, when they make their choice, everyone wins!

Take a moment now and examine if your current process is geared towards offering implementation choices, or if it is based on closing on one specific price. If it is based only on price, identify two further options (price or payment) that will provide additional value, for the client to choose between when agreeing to do business with you.

Summary

In working with sales professionals, I have discovered that many lack a formal selling process. Most spend too little time on the needs analysis, and few take the time to expand their purchasing options in order to provide value based choices to their prospects.

Simply by taking the time to implement this process into your sales presentation, you position yourself as one of the few professionals willing to do what it takes to succeed. Go back now and incorporate this philosophy and process into your business.

Chapter Summary:

1. Always do the pre-requisite intelligence gathering before every call. Know your prospect.
2. Have a prepared agenda for every appointment.
3. Arrive 30 minutes early for every meeting.
4. Be on the lookout for which of the 3 P's is driving the buying decision.
5. "Why do you think this is happening?" *is one of the best needs analysis questions you can ask.*
6. Customers prefer choices and implementation strategies as opposed to being closed.

Chapter 9

Living on the Extra Mile

The extra mile can sometimes seem to be a lonely place because so few people are willing to go there. However, on the extra mile is where all of life's rewards can be found.

At its core, Selling on the Extra Mile is a philosophy for not only selling or conducting business, but for structuring one's entire life. In fact, most of the strategies in this book can be applied to many aspects of one's life beyond that of sales. Choosing to live by this philosophy of doing more than is expected, will quickly elevate the quality of your life better than any method I've ever discovered. All that is required is some extra effort. However, what you will find is that the more energy and effort you invest, the greater your capacity becomes. This is because energy begets more energy and the more you do, the more you can do. We as humans were designed with increasing capacity, and going the extra mile provides the surest path to reaching our full potential.

Let this final chapter be a reminder that sales is holistic, and the practices you developed from this book can be applied to making your entire life successful.

Living on the Extra Mile

In my life, I have been blessed with a handful of teachers who through their conduct, have served as an example of extra mile living. As a result of applying this type of philosophy, they all have lived remarkable lives. One person in particular, stands out as a vivid illustration of what going the extra mile in selling, in your business, and in your life can do for you. His name is Dick Minervino, and I am proud to be his associate, and to be able to call him both my teacher and friend. What makes Dick's life so unique is not just the amazing story of how he rose from abject poverty as a child to a business success; but, also how now at the age of 82 years old, he shows no indication of slowing down. If anything, he has increased his efforts and extended his personal and professional goals far beyond his current achievements.

Dick recounted an incident to me once in which, in his mid-twenties while he was in sales for the telephone company, he had stopped in his hometown for lunch. He was seated at the bar, eating his lunch while reading the book *Think and Grow Rich* by Napoleon Hill. The bartender, who was also someone Dick had known for many years from town, asked him what he was reading. When Dick told him, the bartender, scoffing, asked him, "what are you reading that for?" Dick innocently responded that he intended to become a millionaire. The bartender laughed at him suggesting that Dick could never become a millionaire. Perhaps the bartender was right…because Dick didn't become a millionaire, he went on to become a multi-millionaire, whose fortune continues to grow exponentially with each passing year.

I have been very fortunate to spend much time with Dick, and during our time together he has continued to impart his personal philosophy and strategies for success. One theme that stands out time and again is his willingness to always go that extra mile, as demonstrated by his behavior.

123

Whether it was requesting additional duties as a Marine, taking Dale Carnegie courses in the evenings following work, getting up every morning at 4 AM and not getting home until 10:00 PM that same day as he grew his consulting business, traveling millions of miles across the globe day in and day out to satisfy clients, or taking the time each day to develop his core staff, Dick is a man who has built his home on the Extra Mile.

Multiply your Opportunities

Dick Minervino owns 5 companies encompassing over 100 products and services. He is involved in the growth of each company on a daily basis. Donald Trump, the real-estate mogul, at last count had 50 companies under his umbrella; and Richard Branson, the CEO of Virgin has 300. In all of these cases, these companies provide multiple streams of significant income for their respective owners. On the other end of the spectrum, the average person only has one stream of income, and that is most often their day job.

At a time when the internet has made it possible for everyday people to share their interests and passions with an infinite number of individuals across the planet and earn money for it, most people never bother to learn how. When I ask individuals why they don't put forth the required effort to create an additional income stream, I get the same answer as when I ask them why they don't exercise. The answer usually is, "who has the time?"

However, when we take a closer look at their lives, we discover that they do have the time, it's just being invested in low or no value activities. For example, according to a *2012 A.C. Nielsen Time Use Survey*, the average person watches over 5 hours of TV per day. That is 35 hours per week. Very similar to the amount of time the average employed person spends on the job. If someone was to eliminate TV watching from their life, they would be able to potentially invest the same amount of time they do at work to building their own business.

Jim Rohn, the world famous motivational speaker, said it best, "the first 40 hours of the week are for your survival, the next 40 hours are for your fortune." How much time are you investing in your fortune?

The good news is that the same software tools presented in earlier chapters which can be used to promote your selling business can also be applied to other opportunities. For example, for a very small investment, you can build your own website to showcase your own product or service, you can self-publish a book, sell stuff on eBay, advertise freelance work online, or provide video tutorials via YouTube. The list of possibilities is endless. The only limits are those you put on yourself.

Living on the extra mile means choosing to invest your time in valuable activities that will pay dividends in your future, versus wasting time engaged in mindless activities that will ultimately rob your future.

Go the extra mile in business by deciding now to develop at least one additional stream of income in the next 30 days.

Re-think Retirement

In studying successful individuals and the way that they think, one commonality shows up almost 100% of the time, and that is they practice long term thinking. Long term thinking goes hand in hand with having a vision for your future. A worthy vision is a very powerful tool to guiding your life towards the success you desire. Highly successful people always have a vision for their life, their health, their relationships, their finances, and their business. With the vision firmly set in mind, all of their thoughts are turned toward the horizon where the vision lives, requiring them to think and plan long term. Since it is fundamentally true that our thinking controls our lives, people who concentrate on a vision, and work towards achieving it, often do.

In the Introduction, I wrote how if you are not growing you're dying, and that nothing stays the same in nature. In fact, the universe rewards expansion, and to enjoy all the rewards of life you must constantly be expanding in skills and capabilities.

Setting a vision for yourself where you eventually come to a complete stop in your professional growth and financial growth at age 62 is self-defeating.

In fact, the most successful people I know never think of retiring or stopping, instead are committed to constantly expanding their vision, and manifesting more growth.

Living on the extra mile requires re-thinking your views of retirement. Retirement for many equals decline and death. For instance, how often do where hear about the person that stopped working and then died within just a few years after? On the other hand, discovering work that you love, and endeavoring to do something meaningful with your life that has the potential to leave a legacy, now that is a vision worth living a long life to build.

Although, I am about twenty-five years away from the typical retirement age, I have no intention of retiring. Life is too short to put a finish line on any part of it.

When I talk to most people, they scoff at the idea of not retiring. The reason is that they equate work with bondage, and retirement with freedom. I have always considered myself to be free, and have demonstrated that by taking several short sabbaticals in my life thus far, one that lasted over eight months. Plus, I intend to take more in the future. A sabbatical can be a time to sharpen the saw, to reflect, as well as to plan the achievement of future goals. It is typically during these times that new ideas will emerge. Incorporate sabbaticals in your own life, and let go of the outdated notion of retiring. Retirement was designed for industrial age workers who endured hours of physical, back breaking labor for decades. They retired when their bodies could no longer perform under those conditions. In this golden age of technology and ideas, there is no reason not to plan to provide service (usually called work) for the totality of your life. Everyday then becomes an opportunity to grow, give, and to learn.

Go the extra mile in your life by committing to a life of constant growth and service. Reframe retirement as a time when you will have even more resources to play an even larger game.

Pave the Way

Only leaders can be found on the extra mile. Followers will always be far behind. Those who make the decision to push themselves to do more, accomplish more, and to become more, will always find themselves at the forefront, regardless of their profession.

Salespeople who adhere to the philosophy laid out in this book will become the sales-leaders in their companies and respective businesses. It matters not what your title is, or what your business cards say, every person who applies this philosophy and the strategies it contains eventually emerges to lead in their particular field.

It is the real leaders who naturally get the most rewards in life. What defines a real leader? A real leader leads from the front. They don't ask another to do anything they wouldn't do themselves. In business, the real leaders are close to the customers. By being close to the people they aim to serve, they discover what challenges those individuals are facing, and then in the fashion of true leadership, they go the extra mile to find, or create the solutions those people need. The best products and services have always been created this way. In the same fashion, the best people were forged as they pushed themselves further to make a difference in the lives of the people they touch. When this spreads, as it often does, that is how the world changes for the better. It changes because of people like you...

"Be the change you wish to see in the world." – Gandhi

See you on the Extra Mile!

ABOUT

CHARLES HOUSEHOLDER

Charles Householder is an author and professional speaker. His previous book *Warrior of Life: A Guide to Self-Transformation* is helping people all over the world to change and improve their lives. As a speaker, Householder works with companies of all sizes, teaching and inspiring their employees by sharing his unique philosophies on success, performance, and self-reliance.

In addition to working with companies, Householder delivers public workshops on diverse topics ranging from health and fitness to financial success. He also provides one-on-one, life and business coaching, to individuals. Householder currently resides with his family in Fairfield County, Connecticut. He spends his spare time teaching and practicing the martial arts, participating in endurance events, and working within his community.

HIRE CHARLES HOUSEHOLDER TO SPEAK TO YOUR COMPANY, ASSOCIATION, OR SALES TEAM

Charles Householder regularly delivers comprehensive training based on many of the strategies in this book. He has trained automotive sales professionals, real estate agents, mortgage brokers, and B2B sales professionals from a variety of industries. He is available to provide keynote speeches, and onsite single and multi-day training.

To hire Charles Householder or to for more information please visit:
http://www.charleshouseholder.com.

www.ingramcontent.com/pod-product-compliance
Lightning Source LLC
Chambersburg PA
CBHW051538170526
45165CB00002B/788